Outstretched
FAITH

Outstretched
FAITH

Carmen M. Rodriguez

Xulon Press

Xulon Press
2301 Lucien Way #415
Maitland, FL 32751
407.339.4217
www.xulonpress.com

© 2021 by Carmen M. Rodriguez

All rights reserved solely by the author. The author guarantees all
contents are original and do not infringe upon the legal rights of
any other person or work. No part of this book may be reproduced
in any form without the permission of the author. The views
expressed in this book are not necessarily those of the publisher.

Due to the changing nature of the Internet, if there are any web
addresses, links, or URLs included in this manuscript, these may
have been altered and may no longer be accessible. The views
and opinions shared in this book belong solely to the author and
do not necessarily reflect those of the publisher. The publisher
therefore disclaims responsibility for the views or opinions
expressed within the work.

Unless otherwise indicated, Scripture quotations taken from
the Holy Bible, New Living Translation (NLT). Copyright ©1996,
2004, 2007 by Tyndale House Foundation. Used by permission
of Tyndale House Publishers, Inc.

Paperback ISBN-13: 978-1-6628-2256-8
IeBook SBN-13: 978-1-6628-2257-5

Acknowledgments

** Thank You, Lord Jesus, for creating this. All the glory and honor go to You. You have poured into my mind, heart, and fingers to direct the words that have moved so many hearts. I am humbled and will always be a willing vessel to spread as much as possible about Your goodness and unconditional love.

** I dedicate this book to my children (Stephanie, David Jr., and Joshua) - someone once told me that my purpose in life was to help you all navigate in a world that we know can be so unfair and that all of you would show me compassion. She was right. I love you each so much for your "never giving up" attitude, for your "this is who I am" posture. Always know that I so love you. Be proud of who you are because we are. You do not have to fit in this world; all I want you to know is to stand out for Jesus, who is the only One that defines your identities.

** My husband (David) for understanding, supporting, and trusting what God has placed in my heart to do.

** Thank You, Jesus, for my grandmother (Carmen), who is in heaven with You, for blessing me with her for all the years I had her, and for the wisdom she poured into me, *especially to never give up and to stay strong in the most challenging times.*

** My parents for their support and always believing in me, showing me to go for whatever stirs my heart.

** Grace and Peace Church pastors and church leaders, for your prayers, direction, and support always.

** Grace and Peace Women's Community Group, which was the beginning of this journey. Thank you for your support, encouragement, and sharing the daily text with your families, friends, or co-workers because you believed and trusted that it could make a difference when we share Jesus.

** To all the women who have walked alongside me on my journey. They say it takes a village to raise a child, but it also takes a village to follow the road to Jesus.

Introduction

"Be still, and know that I am God!
I will be honored by every nation.
I will be honored throughout the world."
(Psalm 46:10)

I pray that this book, which God has allowed me to write, uplifts you in a way that you feel encouraged every day as you read each page. May these chapters draw you closer to God to motivate you to know that you are not alone in this journey, but it is a journey we must travel in both the good and hard times. In this journey, we will learn from our Creator, who endured so much on that cross for us. Every day we must choose our battles, but we must always try our best to fight our battles with God's word (yes, scriptures). My favorite verse that you see above has always encouraged me never to give up, that when chaos hits, all we can do is be still in His presence until He calms the storm that tries so hard to drown us. God is always for us and with us; what more can we seek? The answer to every question is calling out His name, looking up, and knowing He sees us and knows the desires in each of our hearts. Enjoy each chapter as it empowers you to remember always who you are and whose you are: God's child. In His stillness, you will find yourself. And once you do, run with it and never look back. Always *remember that our God should be the only One who sits on the throne of our hearts.*

Carmen M. Rodriguez

January 1

My Protector

The LORD is my shepherd; I have all that I need.
(Psalm 23:1)

What does it mean to you that He is our protector? Being led by our shepherd should give you peace of mind because He is our leader, caretaker, protector, provider, and comforter. To be a shepherd takes love, compassion, and a watchful eye for the sheep struggling or losing their way, as they desperately seek to travel the same direction as others. But the shepherd's job is to direct with gentleness as the world rams against the sheep. Being lost is not a bad thing: what is dangerous is staying there. When you look in the Word, you will hear the shepherd's voice. You will learn to listen and hear Him say, "I'm over here. Come. It is okay. Just follow along while I get the other lost sheep." Shepherds do not let go or ever give up. They are always watchful of what can harm a sheep but will also allow them to move freely–to an extent–until they reach a specific boundary, then redirect.

I Shall Not Want

The LORD is my shepherd; I have all that I need.
(Psalm 23:1)

Human flesh pulls us to want more. We think it leads to fulfillment in our lives, that those worldly needs are the answer to contentment. Jesus should be what gives you this contentment. Having God is more significant than what this world can ever offer us. I found this contentment. Choose to be content in who God created you to be (those who genuinely love you will accept you for you), be satisfied with your family, friends, jobs, and whatever else you have, but understand that God does not look at what we have: He looks at our hearts. Search for that contentment in God's presence which offers so much more than the world. Let it fill you with love, grace, peace; let it be ENOUGH to satisfy your life.

January 3

A Place to Lay Down

He lets me rest in green meadows; he leads me beside peaceful streams. (Psalm 23:2)

"Lord Jesus, as a shepherd prepares a place for his sheep to rest, so do You for us." The pasture may have some bumpy patches of obstacles–sin, pride, rebellion, or unforgiveness–but we dig that out and replace it with new seeds of grace, forgiveness, love, peace, and tranquility. It is essential to understand that God wants you to rest. Why? Because how can you serve Him if your body is not sleeping or resting. Life is hard. It drains you, consumes your thoughts, and makes you want to give up. Jesus will prepare for you because He knows what you need and when you need to rest. Stillness is what Jesus wants for us as He works out the details of how He will lead us during our trials. He is the only One in control: of a minor situation up to the most significant difficulty. Jesus is the only One who can give you that spiritual calmness when those waves (people or hardships) are hitting you hard. He knows and leads us out of harmful environments and in the right direction and guides us during hopeless days. When others try to misdirect us, He leads us to be who He wants us to be: people living free, not in fear; in peace, not confused; hopeful, not hopeless; and with a strong faith that will not let anyone take away. Trust Him to lead, and know we are safe along the way. If He goes before us, what can't we overcome?

January 4

Restored Soul

He renews my strength. He guides me along right paths, bringing honor to his name. (Psalm 23:3)

"Thank you, Jesus, for restoration." Sometimes we may ask, how can God restore our lives, mostly when we have shattered pieces? Well, our God is the author of all who restores you and your situation. You go from weak to strong, hopeless to hopeful, sad to filled with joy, and fearful to courageous. See, we cannot change what comes our way, but God will change our hearts and guide us to see life differently with Him next to us. It is like He hits you with lightning, and suddenly, your soul is changed to be better, to seek more, to trust Him alone, and to love unconditionally. May His touch restore peace to your heart, soul, and mind to be better and stronger than before. The beauty in this is He will gently remind you and take you back to when you first encountered Him to ignite the fire inside you again and lead you to that restoration path.

Lead to the Right Way

He renews my strength. He guides me along right paths, bringing honor to his name. (Psalm 23:3)

"Yes, lead us, Jesus, when we sometimes go on the wrong path." We serve a God that always finds us and leads us back to Him. Please make sure you are walking in the direction that will lead to Jesus at the end, not the one with signs of destruction. God is our shepherd, who keeps an eye on us, gives us free will, and picks us up as we get hurt. We are never too far gone. He will call you by your name and direct you back when He sees you entering the danger zone. Sometimes He allows us to enter this danger zone to see how we respond so we learn from it, but then He always pulls us back. To be with Him, we need to run, strive, obey, trust, and allow ourselves to get through obstacles. As we go on righteous paths, we will be training to find peace within our trials and hardships. Who does not want that? God is our Father, but He also has other names that represent His character. Let us look into some: JEHOVAH JIREH (provider) - if you lack, He will make a way to get what you need. JEHOVAH RAPHA (healer) - if you hurt, go to the One that created your heart to find healing. JEHOVAH SHALOM (peace) - no other can give this to you. I am talking about a peace deep in your soul, mind, and heart that you cannot comprehend. Even when the storm comes, it comforts you. It is okay to have tears, but He takes away the fears at that moment. Please look to your shepherd more, and place this in your heart to not forget that He is the only way.

I Need You Beside Me

Even when I walk through the darkest valley, I will not be afraid, for you are close beside me. Your rod and your staff protect and comfort me. (Psalm 23:4)

Fear can be scary when facing danger. Fear will always be a part of us; no one is exempt. At first, it can catch you off guard for a moment. You may panic, get anxious, lose your breath, feel that you have no control of what is happening, or feel at the edge of yourself because of fearful thinking. The Bible says, *"And they have defeated him by the blood of the Lamb and by their testimony. And they did not love their lives so much that they were afraid to die"* (Revelation 12:11). Fear has no control when we have faith. But we must cry out to Him, trust, be who we are, have faith, and open our hearts again to Him. Know that He is safe when others may not be, seek Him and hear His voice. Inhaling courage will remove any fear we may have. Walk with boldness today and know that you will conquer any giant that tries to trip you. When God's presence is in the room, it overwhelms us. Sometimes people need the physical person to believe in Jesus, but He is as present as a physical person if you read His words. As you do, you will feel Him. He will use someone or something to deliver a message to you personally so that He can remind you: "I see you. I have heard every single prayer and have seen your tears. I got you. You are loved." May you feel His presence of peace and assurance of His love as you do your daily task.

It Was not Just a Stick

Even when I walk through the darkest valley, I will not be afraid, for you are close beside me. Your rod and your staff protect and comfort me. (Psalm 23:4)

Just thinking of God's goodness is com-forting. The tangible sticks represent so much then and are also essential now: they represent God's authority, protection, guidance, power, support–something to hold on to when you are about to fall or to move you forward when you are weak. Our shepherd will use these "sticks" to direct us to the narrow righteous path when we are confused about which way to go. Know that straying is not an option for God. He will always gently guide us back to the right path because what He has for us is good, peaceful, and unconditional. Our rod and staff that we carry daily with us (Holy Spirit) is the comfort and freedom we seek. If we let it lead us, we will find what we seek.

January 8

You Got Us Covered

You prepare a feast for me in the presence of my enemies. You honor me by anointing my head with oil. My cup overflows with blessings. (Psalm 23:5)

Hmm, this part can bring some uncom-fortable emotions. When we talk about those who do not like us, we can do nothing but pray for them, forgive them, and not give way to hate. But God always has us covered and prepares a table for whatever the enemy throws at us. God already knows what He will do to keep us safe. Part of the shepherd's job is to protect us, keep an eye out for what or who can hurt us, and remove us from harmful situations. Although sometimes He leaves us at the table with our enemies to show us, we love like Him, and He is God and controls everything and everyone. There is no need to fear because a table prepared is direct access to God and His love. It does not matter who surrounds us; we are safe. A shepherd applies oil on His sheep to protect them, heal wounds, and prevent injuries. For that to happen, the sheep must be still to allow it to be applied. BE STILL, and let God anoint you with His healing hand. King David, when hurt or wounded, went to God for comfort—no one else. It is okay to go to others, but our source is the one that applies the healing touch upon our hearts, protects us when life is not fair and shows us how to prevent injuries to each other. We need to go to our God, submit to His authority over our lives, and be humble as we are in His presence.

January 9

The Cup

You prepare a feast for me in the presence of my enemies. You honor me by anointing my head with oil. My cup overflows with blessings. (Psalm 23:5)

When your cup runs over, that is where you want to be. If you are not there right now, that is okay. Just pray to God to fill you so that as you get filled, it overflows to others. This journey with Him helps you find yourself and overwhelms you so much that you cannot wait to spread Jesus to everyone you encounter. I pray for each of you to overflow with Jesus's peace, love, presence, and blessings. "Lord Jesus, overwhelm us today with that which honors you in our families, friends, church, jobs, and with the ones you will send our way. Thank You for all that You give us each day to survive in a world that can pull us in all different directions. Most importantly, we thank You for Your abundance of unconditional love. Amen."

Waiting To Move To Our Real Home

Surely your goodness and unfailing love will pursue me all the days of my life, and I will live in the house of the LORD forever. (Psalm 23:6)

This world is not our home. He left before us so He can create our own space in His house, and He sent the Comforter (Holy Spirit) to guide us along the way. Peace, faith, and unconditional love will overwhelm us in His house. Our physical body may be here on earth, but our hearts and minds will always be looking forward to the day we will be under the same roof as Jesus. Let us not forget our loved ones who are with Him now that we will also see. Here is a temporary stay, and He is for eternity. Let us go further: if this is not our home, can that be why we are constantly struggling with something in this world? That it feels like something is not correct, and some of us keep searching? We cannot find what we are searching for because what we seek only Jesus can provide. We will never be truly content until we knock on the door of Jesus. No one will ever take care of us like our shepherd (Jesus). He is our peace, our leader, protector, provider, and healer. Be content in Him. He finds us a place of rest when needed. BE STILL in His presence. He restores us from brokenness. Do not fear under Him; be fearless, for He is with you always. He guides and overflows our hearts. He will be with us all of our days, but this is not our home. Remember, this journey is you and Him for a reason. It is not easy at all, but so well worth it. He is molding you to be who He created you to be for His purpose of spreading that He alone offers salvation. It is not about us; it will always be about Him. Keep seeking and NEVER GIVE UP. You will make it–continue holding on, breathe, and look up when hardships come. Let us keep moving.

Reversal Had to Happen

The officer confirmed that Jesus was dead, so Pilate told Joseph he could have the body. (Mark 15:45)

Yes, the cross, let us think about this, the fall of Adam and Eve had to be corrected because that was not God's plan. The only way to fix it was to send Jesus; when He died on that cross, it washed away our sins, and it opened a path to go to God through Him (the only way). He resurrected, showing that death could not hold Him down, that He controls what happened then, what happens now, or what will happen in the future. But we as His children need to help Him by spreading His truth, promises, and hope. Are you doing that? Is that on top of your list or the bottom? We owe God for saving us from further damage and for the sacrifice of Jesus. The cross is that reminder He loves us, and He is for us. With Him, we can conquer anything, but we must have faith and honestly believe it. How will you show you love Jesus today?

Is It My Way or His Way?

The sinful nature wants to do evil, which is just the opposite of what the Spirit wants. And the Spirit gives us desires that are the opposite of what the sinful nature desires. These two forces are constantly fighting each other, so you are not free to carry out your good intentions. (Galatians 5:17)

Isn't this our battle? Don't we live according to our way until it gets out of control and then cry out to Him to do things His way? I once heard that whatever decisions or promises we make should ultimately help keep us on track or direct us back whenever we are confused in situations. If we decide to follow and trust God, we must remember that He saved us to remind us who we serve when temptation comes. We have a daily choice: to love or to hate, to be distant or to hug, to say hi or to walk away, to judge or to have compassion. But it is hard to choose between what we see versus what we do not. Thank God for that conflict within us that I know has kept us out of trouble many times. As I said yes to Him, I had to learn that all of my steps adjusted to His way more as soon as I said, "Help me." The conflict within stops as soon as we remember to dwell in His presence. He always wins.

No Drama

In every place of worship, I want men to pray with holy hands lifted up to God, free from anger and controversy. (1 Timothy 2:8)

When we worship God, may we understand that it is Holy ground (in His presence, peace, serenity, love)? When we praise Him with our hands lifted, may we realize that we are free from anything that disturbs our minds (disagreements, the war of words, bickering, quarreling)? These distractions will apply to our relationships with others; the enemy loves when he can break a marriage, friendships, families, relationships with co-workers, fellow church members, etc. Why? Because if the enemy can break you here, it takes away your peace and distracts you from focusing on Jesus. So, FLIP it: decide you will do what you can do with the help of Jesus to keep peace with everyone; if anything arises that disturbs this peace, pray first, address it, and make things right. Do not let anyone get in your way of being right with Jesus. It is your journey and peace of mind.

January 14

Sacrifice for Him

The sacrifice you desire is a broken spirit. You will not reject a broken and repentant heart, O God. (Psalm 51:17)

If you read the verse, God wants us to sacrifice our will and give Him authority to take over everything; He knows what it will mean for us–whether it offers time or energy daily, weekly, or biweekly. But see it this way: we should want our mindset to go above and beyond. Do we want blessings to be overflowing, more than just a weekly gift? Make the sacrifice to be in His presence. He is waiting. He never turns away. He knows the tray of sufferings we all have experienced, not just now but even childhood arrows that try to attack us. So here it goes: hear Him say, "I'm sorry for what you went through. I was there with you. Everyone has free will, but that does not define who you are now. You are my daughter. You are first in my eyes. You mattered even when others made you think you did not. I am sorry you had to be an adult when you should have been a child. I love you, which is why I sacrificed for you."

Fighting Spirit

This is my command—be strong and courageous! Do not be afraid or discouraged. For the LORD your God is with you wherever you go." (Joshua 1:9)

We cannot ever forget to honor those serving the United States of America to keep us safe and remember those who did before and lost their lives for us. We ask for God to be with all the families now who supported the ones who sacrificed. Having a fighting spirit is being in a position of never giving up, persevering even when it looks impossible or hurts. This spirit is true especially for our loved ones fighting during health complications: they are FIGHTERS. It is easy to give up during battles–temptation, sickness, trials–or when others whisper words of discouragement because they lost their fighting without God. You see, maybe that is what the world says. But God says to be strong and courageous, have no fear, follow the Word, and stand firm. He will be with us wherever we go. Keep fighting the battles because someone needs you to be present, support, and love them through.

We Are to Serve

So Jesus called them together and said, "You know that the rulers in this world lord it over their people, and officials flaunt their authority over those under them. But among you it will be different. Whoever wants to be a leader among you must be your servant, and whoever wants to be first among you must be the slave of everyone else. For even the Son of Man came not to be served but to serve others and to give his life as a ransom for many." (Mark 10:42-45)

Yes, the Prince of Peace, Jesus served others no excuses for us not to unless we are not ready to commit to this walk or do not want to reach others who are hopeless. You see, all our purposes will be connected to serving others, whether it is another believer or unbeliever, because that is what He expects from us. Serving is not just physical; it is understanding, encouraging others along the way to find the path of life, hope, and identity. Some struggle with serving? Ask God where He wants you. Ask Him to show you. And if someone wants to serve you, that is a blessing from God. Jesus helped by teaching, healing, walking the walk because His purpose on earth was to come down to experience what we would go through so that He would serve us better.

He is our example of handling this world and equips us to be overcomers and stay obedient as we humbly serve with unconditional hearts.

January 17

Trusting Hearts

This is what the LORD says: "Cursed are those who put their trust in mere humans, who rely on human strength and turn their hearts away from the LORD. (Jeremiah 17:5)

We are not to trust our flesh. We cannot put our confidence in the flesh, as this is what gets us in trouble all the time unless the Holy Spirit has overpowered it for its purpose. So, what am I saying? Confidence in the Holy Spirit allows us always to let the Holy Spirit direct our moves, feelings, minds, hearts, and steps. If our flesh has a part to play, may it be for purposes to hold ones who need it, help others along their journey, pray to our God or be ready to serve when God calls us? Our hearts belong to the Holy Spirit and no one else. Being in tune with Jesus allows Him to take control and shield us with the breastplate of righteousness. It is free from any burden that can come our way. If a conflict gets through because the flesh took over, take your hand, place it over your heart; endure the pain, but be soothed by the Holy Spirit.

January 18

Right Beside Him

No, O people, the LORD has told you what is good, and this is what he requires of you: to do what is right, to love mercy, and to walk humbly with your God. (Micah 6:8)

Walk HUMBLY with Him. It is that simple comfort, that honors, that love, that bonding time with Him alone - no interruptions, no worries, no judgment. Just soaking all He has for us, all He needs for us to do for Him, all He wants to teach us if we only focus on Him and not the worldly things. To walk with Him should be an honor, not an obligation. Why do we sometimes feel being in His presence is a burden when He is the answer to all our issues? He is a gentleman, unlike any other, who can show us what it is to be unconditionally loved, truly forgiven, and understood. I pray we all feel His presence—whether everything seems good or when it is falling apart. If you are lost or have strayed away, I say run to find Him and get Him next to you again. All we need is Him. It is nice to have others, but sometimes He works better in us when we spend time with Him alone.

Set Apart (Different/Special)

"I knew you before I formed you in your mother's womb. Before you were born I set you apart and appointed you as my prophet to the nations." *(Jeremiah 1:5)*

As I saw my son walk across the room after graduating, we had a moment when we just looked at each other and smiled. His accomplished look said, "I did it," and mine said, "Thank You, God, for him. I knew you would do it." Why am I sharing? Because God has a path for everyone. Some tracks will take us a different route, but they will eventually end up in the same destination. God sets each of us apart for a reason. Maybe we cannot handle specific paths now, or He had to adjust before we step on a track because His will requires it. Bumps and bruises we get are worth it and unavoidable as we go on our ways because it is all for Him. We all want to be seen by God. Be the real you as you walk this journey. Those who genuinely love you will accept your imperfections that only your Creator can change if He wants to. If not, they lose the blessing of YOU in their lives.

January 20

Blessings Taken Away

But Isaac said, "Your brother was here, and he tricked me. He has taken away your blessing." (Genesis 27:35)

One brother took another brother's blessing from the father. The enemy is the culprit for encouraging this to happen. The enemy is the one who would and could take away what God has for us if we are not careful. We must be prayed up and pour ourselves in the Word to be covered. We all have experienced these temporarily lost blessings due to not being obedient to God. Notice I said "temporarily" because our God will still bless us when we get back on track. Maybe it was not what He originally had for us, but whatever He gives is good, on time, and what we need instead of what we want unless it is His will. He blesses the righteous, the ones who search with sincere and faithful hearts, the selfless, the humble, and those who do not waver no matter the cost.

Build Up or Break Down

But you should keep a clear mind in every situation. Don't be afraid of suffering for the Lord. Work at telling others the Good News, and fully carry out the ministry God has given you. (2 Timothy 4:5)

Demanding circumstances are a part of life. Some we are indirectly affected by, and others we are responsible for causing. But God sometimes may give us events that are challenging to teach us a lesson. It will destroy us if we ignore or do not address these situations. The result is dependent on how we respond. As you read, it says, have a clear mind in every case (yes, hear Jesus). Have no fear in moments of suffering, for God is with you. Not everyone will understand unless they have that encounter with Jesus. Spread the Word to all you encounter, and do His will that has been assigned to you specifically. If you have not taken these steps, what is holding you back in going forward? Jesus carried this out for us.

Out of the Trenches

For he will conceal me there when troubles come; he will hide me in his sanctuary. He will place me out of reach on a high rock. (Psalm 27:5)

Trenches (shelter from enemy attack or a place to be temporarily protected). Does this sound familiar? When challenging moments come, we have to jump into the trenches but understand being in this place was not to shut down and allow all those emotions to overwhelm us; it was to get prepared for what is next, but God covers us. Trenches are helpful and needed. We need to think of strategies on how or what to do when we must come out as we apply this now. Yes, it is different, but here we are reminded God covers His people, hides them from attacks; yes, some will get injured. If you read above this verse, it states even if King David feels afraid - he will remain confident, and so shall we. Some will fight through, and some will be confused or scared. Others will strive to the next thing God is assigning – yes, stay focused on Him, we win whether in trenches or not.

January 23

Right Perspective

And we know that God causes everything to work together for the good of those who love God and are called according to his purpose for them. (Romans 8:28)

What is the proper perspective to have in your life? Ask God to help you understand, especially the part that says, "everything" and "those who love God." Again, not half or a third but everything. What am I saying? Think of where you are right now in current situations that are challenging WHO YOU ARE. I pray that as problems arise that you see His perspective, not yours. I pray that you see His truth. After all, as we see things through our own eyes, our vision becomes blurry because we let our hearts take over instead of looking up and staying focused on Jesus. It is true: your weakness will be used against you by the enemy. Fight that with scriptures that protect your mind, heart, and thoughts. We have the weapons in our hands, but sometimes we forget we have the power to use them. Ask God if it aligns with Him. If it does not, then wait. Waiting does not mean you stay stagnant–run after God in the Word, worship, and in prayer.

What is Fellowship?

Therefore, since we are surrounded by such a huge crowd of witnesses to the life of faith, let us strip off every weight that slows us down, especially the sin that so easily trips us up. And let us run with endurance the race God has set before us. (Hebrews 12:1)

Do you fellowship with your circumstances or with God? Wow, we do not think we do this, but sometimes we do. The more we focus on our afflictions, the bigger they become, and the smaller God seems. Something is not suitable if we are always in that position. Flip it: GOD is greater; never less. He is not second; we are. He is first above anybody or anything in our lives. Please do not change the order. If you have, then you have your answer to your problems. May you meet with God and share your heart. He sees you–believe it. He knows your strengths and weaknesses, for you are His Beloved. Isn't that comforting to know? Remember who is behind your struggles and keeps you discouraged or down. He may start it, but remember God always WINS. Just pray to Him and watch Him throw His best shot at the enemy.

January 25

Heart

God blesses those whose hearts are pure, for they will see God. (Matthew 5:8)

Visualize this when you think of your heart: you have layers of covering. The first layer is thick to protect against any damage. Then, as you go deeper, you pass through thinner layers, then you enter that place that only Jesus resides and works through you, that place that keeps you going even when you feel you cannot anymore. Obstacles come at you all at once as you are waiting for God to give you a clue. But that is your safe place. Those thin layers result from difficult moments as you got closer to Him. He worked through your thick layers. Trusting, doing right, loving, forgiving, trying, praying, changing, hoping, and having faith. He changed us. These are the hearts He wants: the pure ones, not the perfect ones. The ones who genuinely repent their sins and keep going in the right direction even when obstacles come. Who is leading your heart?

Who Does not Want to be in God's Waiting Room?

My future is in your hands. Rescue me from those who hunt me down relentlessly. (Psalm 31:15)

Waiting is not easy unless you have already been through the process of it and know it requires patience, trust, and faith. But God's timing never fails. He already has what He wants for us, but we need to grow in some areas before revealing it to us. He only expects obedience, trust, faith, a tenacious attitude, and a willing heart, even if you do not get it. I pray that He reveals to you what you could not see in your situation before so that you know He sees you, knows, gets it, and most importantly, He loves you. Yes, YOU. Your time is in His hands because we all belong only to Him. Remember, the enemy does not have any control unless you give him the authority.

January 27

Anticipating Change

She had heard about Jesus, so she came up behind him through the crowd and touched his robe. (Mark 5:27)

This story is of a woman who bled for 12 years and stopped as soon as she touched Jesus's robe. Her faith is what made her well. She was willing to do what was needed to get healed, mind you, of what she had endured from others. Her physical reaching out is the same as having the mindset to reach out to Him even with the emotional, mental, and physical pains. Reading scripture is a way of wading through crowds to capture Jesus's robe. It does not matter who is watching when you are praising and crying out to God, asking for healing, or searching for answers. Even if you must wait 12 years, your faith is the only thing that will get you through. He is still working in you in the waiting period, but you need to be in His presence to see and feel it. Remember, when you see others receive their blessings, be encouraged because it gives you hope that He will do the same for all His faithful followers, but at His timing.

Jesus Knows

"Simon, Simon, Satan has asked to sift each of you like wheat. But I have pleaded in prayer for you, Simon, that your faith should not fail. So when you have repented and turned to me again, strengthen your brothers." (Luke 22:31-32)

As you read, Peter denies Jesus three times. Have you ever been there or denied more than that? If you read further, you will see three factors during denial:

** Concern for his image.
** Hanging with the wrong crowd (guards) created a shift in identity (he even said he did not know Him).
** Following from a distance.

Was he ashamed? Fearful? Did he not want to be associated with Jesus at the moment? This process was because Jesus prayed for him that faith would not fail in the midst of what was going on. He knew he would repent and that he had faith, but it needed to be worked on to take him to the next level. To encourage others, just like us, we get to the next level, but our faith will be the key. It is not easy but hang on. If all you have at the end of the day is JESUS, you gained the best. You did not lose. Remember that.

Fight, Follow, Faithful

Fight the good fight for the true faith. Hold tightly to the eternal life to which God has called you, which you have declared so well before many witnesses. (1 Timothy 6:12)

If we read about Paul, we see that he went through a lot and was determined to finish well because he knew the One he served would be worth it. Life can feel like hills (elevated issues come up unexpectedly) and like valleys (problems not as intense but still challenging). If you read about valleys, they usually have a river that flows through them. Yes, you know where I am going with this. We fight with prayers and verses when we need to. We follow the narrow path, so we finish well. We may walk alone, but God is before us, and we know that someone will be behind us to make sure we keep going. Never give up and stay faithful to Him. Through our hills and valleys, He promises to be with us through it all and that we will not be overwhelmed by them. Finish well; the prize for the righteous is waiting.

January 30

Our Journey

But God showed his great love for us by sending Christ to die for us while we were still sinners. (Romans 5:8)

This race that God gives us comes with grace. Thank God for the moments He gave you grace when you knew deep down you did not deserve it or when you did not expect it. Remember to pass that grace to others. No, it is not easy, but God never said it was going to be. I am so thankful for how God's presence in our journeys overwhelms us. Know this: God's timing never fails. Keep running this race. Do not stop; keep praying, reading, seeking, hearing about Jesus, and most importantly, sharing who He is. Do not be ashamed or silent, child of God, when you have a chance to share about Him to those searching, mostly lost friends or family.

Pursue Me Above All

The LORD looks down from heaven on the entire human race; he looks to see if anyone is truly wise, if anyone seeks God. (Psalm 14:2)

We can sometimes pursue (go after, follow something or someone to catch them) so many things except Jesus. Or we did seek Him, but somehow, once we saw Him, it wasn't fun, exciting, or overflowing of love anymore? Because of the expectations that we know are put on us, we stop seeking, which leads to a lack of growth in our faith. I am not saying that someone does not believe, but what I am saying is that if we constantly seek temporary fulfillment, why wouldn't we seek the forever satisfaction of Jesus? He "looks down to see if any is truly wise," says the verse. Do not waste time; seek Him and stay there. Hold on, especially in your moments of hardship, because that is the only place you will find the strength and peace that no one else can give. Make sure you do not look to anything or anyone else as your God.

Do Not Stray

My dear brothers and sisters, if someone among you wanders away from the truth and is brought back, you can be sure that whoever brings the sinner back from wandering will save that person from death and bring about the forgiveness of many sins. (James 5:19-20)

We always hear not to stray (separate, move away from something right for us, or drift). Holding on is not easy in a world that makes what is terrible for us seem so right. But the question is, does it have Jesus in it? If it does not, that is why we stray. It is not because of Him, for He never leaves us; however, we want what we want and know He will be right where we left Him waiting for us to come back. We assume even if we get consequences that it will excuse our behavior. But what do we get from straying? No peace, no identity, stuck in a grey area, distanced from ones who genuinely accept us for who we are. Just like with Jesus, we think they will be there when we come back. Sometimes that is the case, and other times we lose the good to pursue the bad. In the same way, pray for the ones you love to come back, be patient, let them go through the process, and love them anyway because no one gets left behind.

February 2

Find Peace

And let the peace that comes from Christ rule in your hearts. For as members of one body you are called to live in peace. And always be thankful. (Colossians 3:15)

If there is no God in the core of your heart, how can there be peace? How can we make it through each day? God is not only love, hope, faith, serenity, and tranquility, but He is also PEACE. The Bible says to make every effort to make peace. We know this is hard, especially when it is our intention but not well received by others. We must not give up for others the peace we seek in Jesus. What do I mean? Make peace as much as we can; it will either be received or not. Do it because God says so, and if we want to be close to God, we need to do it. Do not look for the response of others. He knows our hearts, especially the pain we feel when we lose those that do not want to maintain peace. We cannot do anything but pray for them and take care of our temples. He wants us with a peaceful heart, mind, and soul.

February 3

Spread Your Seeds

And the seed that fell on good soil represents those who hear and accept God's word and produce a harvest of thirty, sixty, or even a hundred times as much as had been planted!" (Mark 4:20)

The seed is God's word. Yes, we are to share who He is. Yes, we are to share our testimonies. Why this is so important is because no one can tell your story but you. Others watch us through our storms and wonder how we made it through without drowning. We need to wait for that seed to grow deeper in others' hearts. Of course, it is not easy, as all we can do is spread but not embed in them to understand what they are missing. We can let them know that this seed is the answer they seek. Seeds make it to people's hearts, some are taken and given to the enemy, and some are looked at and stored away. "Lord Jesus, give us as many seeds as possible to spread to others who seek. If the soil (heart) is hard, soften it, and let the seed fall into the cracks, so that if something moves, it intensifies like never before. Amen."

February 4

Book

All Scripture is inspired by God and is useful to teach us what is true and to make us realize what is wrong in our lives. It corrects us when we are wrong and teaches us to do what is right. (2 Timothy 3:16)

We search for the perfect book on what to do in our lives, but we already have the only "Book" we need (yes, the Bible). Everything we have experienced and will experience in the future is there. Its purpose is to teach, help, correct, and show how to live. The world makes us feel that if we are on God's path, we miss out on something, but so what? Our salvation, peace, faith, and hope in Jesus are more important. Temporary entertainment with worldly things that do not pour into our souls will not get us closer to Jesus. It will just push you further away. What am I saying? Make the time to explore the Bible. Let it correct you, break you, heal you, unconditionally love you, identify you, speak to who you are (wonderfully made), and help you BE that person. It is God's word that pierces our hearts, and we know it is in our best interest. God is in front of us always, and we know His words will guide our lives.

Honor Him

"Do not be afraid, for I am with you. I will gather you and your children from east and west. I will say to the north and south, 'Bring my sons and daughters back to Israel from the distant corners of the earth. Bring all who claim me as their God, for I have made them for my glory. It was I who created them.'" (Isaiah 43:5-7)

All for His glory; that is our goal in life. So, what does this mean? How would you interpret this for your existence here and now? Well, we must ask: are we making steps to get to know Him daily? He offers so much wisdom, but do we believe in who He says He is or giving the enemy the power to confuse or discourage us? Or are we too broken to even try again? Be encouraged, for He is option A. No other option is needed. Keep praying, striving, and stretching that hand because you will rise. Some may need a push, which is okay. It is better than standing in the same position or giving the enemy a chance to knock you down again. We must know God's character. Yes, YOU. So, let us pray, seek, run, move, invest time, and shout for Him as we do for other things that are temporary satisfaction but do not bring salvation, love, and peace.

February 6

The Temple

Don't you realize that your body is the temple of the Holy Spirit, who lives in you and was given to you by God? You do not belong to yourself, for God bought you with a high price. So you must honor God with your body. (1 Corinthians 6:19-20)

The Bible says the Holy Spirit lives in us (the temple), so yes, physically, we should try to take care of our bodies. It is not easy, as emotions or mindsets can stress the body, but somehow, we must protect this temple from any harm. It honors God; it grieves when we grieve, it is the place that stores the strength we need, a place that guides, directs, corrects, protects, and understands us. I think Jesus knew we could not survive without Him, so He gave us the Holy Spirit. We should be honored. How many times has life been unfair, with no one around but the comfort of Jesus that got us through? The verse says we do not belong to ourselves, so why do we try to bury the Holy Spirit deep down and allow others to control our temples? Only One sacrificed for us and deserved all the glory and honor.

Will You Follow?

But Ruth replied, "Don't ask me to leave you and turn back. Wherever you go, I will go; wherever you live, I will live. Your people will be my people, and your God will be my God. (Ruth 1:16)

A parable of two women not related only by marriage, although they both suffered loss, Ruth would not leave her mother-in-law, Naomi. The words of "Wherever you go, I will go." What does that mean to you in your relationship with God and others? Let us apply it to our lives. Are we close to saying this to God, wherever you go, God, I will go? Or in our relationships? It is heartfelt for someone to say this because we give up ourselves. After all, they mean that much, or they are all we have. God is our all first, and if we follow Him, then we will be able to follow or be there for all those people we care for to the capacity that they may need us to be, but are we willing to invest the time and effort it takes, not everyone does or can handle other's burdens. Still, with God directing, we can, as He is the one that orchestrates who will be in their journey to help them keep going.

Run for Jesus

We do this by keeping our eyes on Jesus, the champion who initiates and perfects our faith. Because of the joy awaiting him, he endured the cross, disregarding its shame. Now he is seated in the place of honor beside God's throne. (Hebrews 12:2)

Our journey as Christians can be chal-lenging. We are sinners, but because of Jesus, we have salvation. He was the gap between God and us. No good deed, no award, no gift, or money will give us eternal life: a race of emotions, questions, confusion, and constant praying. What am I saying? More was done on the cross than we could ever do. God has made each of our paths not wide but narrow. You will encounter pillars of bondages that will fall, but you will get through with your faith as you run, walk, or crawl. Do whatever you can, but do not give up. Keep moving even if you are at the edge of yourself and you feel alone. Keep your eyes on Jesus: your focus, your finish line, your strength, your motivation, and your joy. And in this race, be ready to pick up others along the way because we encourage others just the same.

Defeated He Will Be

Then the devil, who had deceived them, was thrown into the fiery lake of burning sulfur, joining the beast and the false prophet. There they will be tormented day and night forever and ever. (Revelation 20:10)

Jesus said, "It is finished," we should be satisfied with that, but somehow, some are not convinced. We win all battles, but we must be strong, focused, driven, and unshakable. The enemy knows how to make the vulnerable weak, but we are allowing him that opportunity. We need to get to the point that when we get up and walk with our God-given and driven authority, the enemy says and knows, "She or he is up and alert. I need to be careful today." As he stalks to destroy, we need to see those moves and be prepared and remember we have the Holy Spirit that alerts us. We get distracted that we do not see the enemy coming, which allows him to invade our minds and weakness. Yes, the weapons against us are the ones we give the enemy, so do not.

February 10

Friendship Extended

The king then asked him, "Is anyone still alive from Saul's family? If so, I want to show God's kindness to them." Ziba replied, "Yes, one of Jonathan's sons is still alive. He is crippled in both feet." (2 Samuel 9:3)

We have talked about the friendship of King David and Jonathan. They genuinely loved, respected, and protected each other. A faithful love was the promise that King David vowed to treat Jonathan's family. It will show in our friendships; we will see and know who takes us or not by how they love those connected to us. When they promised each other, God blessed it, but most importantly, because He was there, that is why the relationship was always strong and overcame the challenging obstacles. God's plan was for a time as this as Jonathan's disabled son Mephibosheth would need help, King David would be the one to take him in. Thank God for those who are genuinely for us, love the ones important to us, and give us a helping hand when needed.

February 11

Trust/Afraid

I trust in God, so why should I be afraid? What can mere mortals do to me? (Psalm 56:11)

There is no perfect being but God, so knowing that should comfort all of us. There is no bar to try to measure up to except the one that leads to Jesus. Yes, we are who we are–no comparing–each with a gift from God, so until you activate it or figure it out, know either way He loves us through our imperfections, insecurities, disorganized thoughts, and even when we worry. He loves us because we are keeping it real; there is no faking in front of Him. You must take the layers of self-off to show the real YOU. He knows those deep-rooted, secret areas that can creep up on us for a moment until a spoken word from Him through someone or a song played brings us back to stand firm in our faith. You gain confidence when you finally realize who you are in Him. Fear can block our faith if we allow it but walk with COURAGE.

February 12

A Pledge

It is God who enables us, along with you, to stand firm for Christ. He has commissioned us, and he has identified us as his own by placing the Holy Spirit in our hearts as the first installment that guarantees everything he has promised us. (2 Corinthians 1:21-22)

Here it goes, we surrender all of us, and we get Jesus – who takes everything that we give and makes the best decisions for us, but somehow we decide later the things we ask for Him to take care of we take it back, and we get back to our old cycle. Jesus is real as anyone in this world. Why is it hard to grasp it, trust it, or only say His name for our convenience? I heard you do not use His name if we are not going to do His walk, ouch, was my reaction, but it makes sense if we are not in it fully don't disrespect His name as a cliché, slogan, it sounds good or for some it will attract people but for personal gain, not God gain, keeping it real. He took us seriously and made a promise, and invited us to follow, trust, walk, and believe in Him so we can find peace. He sealed and gave us the Holy Spirit as that pledge. Today find your genuine commitment to Him as you say – "JESUS."

Misdirected Thinking

I know what enthusiasm they have for God, but it is misdirected zeal. (Romans 10:2)

We all should know that anyone that does not believe in the Only way (Jesus) will not be saved or go to heaven; this is for all people included. Israel does love God but has allowed misled thinking to lose sight of what is right in front of them. This zeal (eagerness, passion, enthusiasm, and pursuit of something) is somehow not in following God's way. If anyone has experienced this is beautiful in our walk with Jesus, this zeal keeps us well connected to Him, wanting that time to find peace in all areas of life. Is the thinking I will follow tomorrow, or are we busy entertaining others that may not care about our souls? If we get counsel from someone who is not walking right with Jesus - be careful. A true friend is not going along, so friendship is not lost. It is helping them find their way to Jesus, who will make them obedient in helping find that zeal.

Giving Up Our Will

Seek his will in all you do, and he will show you which path to take. (Proverbs 3:6)

Quite simply, if we want the right direction, path, peace, or contentment, seek Him, run after Him, find Him, put everything we have into His will, His people, and His purpose. But yes, it will be a challenge; anything we want to attain will have a cost, a sacrifice of the heart, or will require us to work. We gain a path with Jesus, new friends, we get clarity where we may be confused, and an approach to walking with Him to serve others (another benefit if you genuinely love to help people. Not everyone does). Seeking God's will moves us to His ways of accomplishing the mission, not ours, no matter our thoughts or feelings. Put everything into His will with faith and obedience no matter what, and the promise is He will show us the right path to what is the best for us, but we must do our part daily to find Him, please find Him.

The Power of Sisterhood

We know what real love is because Jesus gave up his life for us. So we also ought to give up our lives for our brothers and sisters. (1 John 3:16)

God gives us sisterhood to help with healing in areas of struggle. Sisterhood is spiritual food and natural food. It is talking about real issues–hard but true–backed up with what the Bible says, to love, forgive, heal, and withhold judgment. But the truth is, we all have been broken, struggled, or pondered on the deep, spiritual questions. We must hold each other up by holding each other accountable. Sometimes you may not like what you hear or may not like what others say, but there is respect in giving each other that authority to help when needed because they got you, and you love them. Those are the ones I know I want and need in my life and will not let go of them. It will keep you focused, confident, humble, and REAL with yourself and them.

Most Important One

Anyone who wanders away from this teaching has no relationship with God. But anyone who remains in the teaching of Christ has a relationship with both the Father and the Son. (2 John 9)

We all have relationships with so many people. All are important, all are different, and all take work. Yes, a lot of compromises are needed, and all relationships need God at the center. If you take out God, those relationships will struggle. It is like you are lost as you wander away. But let us go further: the first connection we have is Jesus, who waits for us to call Him when we are in trouble. In the same way, we pour into our relationships; we also need to take care of our relationship with Jesus. Seek Him, lean on Him, and run to Him, even when He feels far. Know this: He is always there. We are the ones who create distance–not purposely, not intentionally–we just get distracted by other people or just life. What is the point? Take care of the central relationship in your life, and all others will fall in place. All others will find direction, unconditional love, forgiveness, compassion, understanding, compromise, and restoration.

February 17

Accountable To Him

Yes, each of us will give a personal account to God. (Romans 14:12)

We are all accountable to God. It should keep us on our toes. But He also sends our friends or sisters, who care enough to be part of our lives and world, who accept who we are, who offer their advice as best as they can without judgment. It is essential and needed on your journey, and God sends the ones who will stand by your side and challenge you with unconditional love and who you can hold up as well. Accountability encourages and makes you feel loved. It is security, and it is acceptance of who you are; it is trust. You will know who to pick to hold you accountable in your words or actions, or God will send one, and it will motivate you because you are not alone.

February 18

What is the Struggle?

Faith shows the reality of what we hope for; it is the evidence of things we cannot see. (Hebrews 11:1)

If God controls all, then we must step forward and trust. Is it easy? No. Some are so afraid to trust that they included God in that "do not trust" list without realizing that He is the only truly trusted friend we will ever have. In those scary moments, so many things come our way, but if we say we believe, we say He is our God, then those moments are when our faith must come out stronger and louder than ever before. Do we genuinely believe, or are we like some who say it but do not follow through in a real sense? In or out? Do not struggle anymore when you give up control and have no more expectations except the expectation to be in Jesus's presence. There are surprises but blessings, not bondages. This verse expresses, "I will trust in You even though I can't see you, Jesus." Yes, even if we do not know for sure if a step is a wise one, we know He will say if we are in tune with Him, "Take a bigger step. You are on the right path."

February 19

Jesus's Lasso

We destroy every proud obstacle that keeps people from knowing God. We capture their rebellious thoughts and teach them to obey Christ. (2 Corinthians 10:5)

So, we know a lasso is a rope you use to capture something. When Jesus captures us, it is when we are about to get ourselves in trouble or going in the opposite direction. The beauty of it is that He cares enough to take the time to capture us. What do we do? Do we fight it? Or were we waiting to be grabbed because we were tired? Do we allow God to pull us toward Him? Do we apologize to God for having to get a lasso even to capture our attention? Yes, just like Wonder Woman's lasso when she grabbed people, they could not move and would have to admit the truth. It captured their thoughts. They had to decide on how to react or respond. Being captured by Jesus is an honor: we do not have to walk alone anymore. Let Jesus lead to help put you back on track. Surrender.

February 20

A Permeated Movement

He also asked, "What else is the Kingdom of God like? It is like the yeast a woman used in making bread. Even though she put only a little yeast in three measures of flour, it permeated every part of the dough." (Luke 13:20-21)

The one main requirement is a little yeast (a little faith, mustard seed) to spread and fill up every part of the bread. If we apply this to life, we will spring into motion the same spreading of Jesus to others. Some may think more is needed of us, but that is not true. Why? Because He chooses us and takes care of us, and in return, we need to trust, hope, and love with what we have at the moment. Eventually, it will permeate (spread) within us and then out of us to others. We all belong to the Kingdom of God. Daily that little yeast (our faith) rises as we search for His guidance, and once we find it, it completes who we are. It produces an overflow of Jesus to spread to all parts of God's Kingdom. Take ownership of your piece of this big puzzle. Know that you are needed, and your uniqueness is essential.

February 21

Rock

All of them ate the same spiritual food, and all of them drank the same spiritual water. For they drank from the spiritual rock that traveled with them, and that rock was Christ. (1 Corinthians 10:3-4)

Remember that sometimes when our cup is getting empty, we need to try our best to pour into ourselves the only One that can hold us together. You may not mean to be at that point, but sometimes life can storm so hard that it depletes your cup of strength and takes you to what was within you that identifies you. Yes, that Rock is Jesus. As soon as we feel it slipping, we hold on tighter because that is what keeps us focused, determined, unwavering, and walking with clarity. Visualize a stack of rocks. It is like our life: we need to be patient as we stack each one and find the balance to all be there but do not fall. All of what Jesus has put in us reminds us that storms may come, but you keep your balance and do not give up.

Know Your Source That Drives Your Heart

But God knew what would happen, and his prearranged plan was carried out when Jesus was betrayed. With the help of lawless Gentiles, you nailed him to a cross and killed him. (Acts 2:23)

What drives you to act, to move, or to love? Jesus was part of God's deliberate plan. Yes, we may say we know, but what if we ponder on that for a minute? Let it go deep to the core of your heart, and this should be what drives our being. He should never be put away for anyone. When we genuinely decide and understand His purpose was to come to help us, we find the source that moves us at speed too fast to control. Strip away all barriers in your mind–yes, even the one that seems to be the toughest–and give to Jesus. Lean into Him. If not, we drown in the storms surrounding us. The world throws, but you need to throw back as hard as you can. It is like lifting weights: the more added to you, the stronger you will get by adjusting your mind and positioning yourself to push back even through the pain. Jesus is helping the whole time. Go for it, Warriors.

Losing Battle

But they rebelled against him and grieved his Holy Spirit. So he became their enemy and fought against them. (Isaiah 63:10)

If we are not fighting with the Spirit, we will never win. Even when we are against others, we never really win with our words or actions. When we go against others, something within happens. We grieve. Pain, hurt, extreme distress, and heartbreak strikes us. Because of the Holy Spirit, we cannot ignore this. How can we? Knowing that being saved keeps us more in tune with those feelings, we did not seem to have before. Jesus gets hit first (Didn't He suffer enough?) by our actions. Then the ones who have offended us get hit with our words that wound them as well. Finally, we are hurt as they come against us with their words. Who wins? So here it goes: try to make right what grieves Jesus, then everything will be correct. You will feel the difference in your soul. You will feel peace, stillness, better sleep, and more focus. We need Jesus to be our friend, not our enemy.

February 24

Into His Hands

Then Jesus shouted, "Father, I entrust my spirit into your hands!" And with those words he breathed his last. (Luke 23:46)

Yes, He died for all of us. He loves all of us. We believe that our sins, if we genuinely repent to God, are forgiven and that He will never leave us. When Jesus died, He entrusted His spirit into God's hands. So, we should give Him full responsibility, trust, and the right to protect us whichever way He chooses. That does not mean it will not sometimes hurt because it will. Especially when He must discipline us or when we must suffer the consequences. But He is God, in whose better hands do you want to be holding you? The cross reminds us of forgiveness, sacrifice, and broken bondages (we must pick ourselves back up). A sinless man paid for our sins: His love is unconditional, and nothing that we have done will ever change that. Our old self is gone. We have a new beginning, hope, faith, and VICTORY.

February 25

Walking or Running Toward Your Purpose

So I run with purpose in every step. I am not just shadowboxing. I discipline my body like an athlete, training it to do what it should. Otherwise, I fear that after preaching to others I myself might be disqualified. (1 Corinthians 9:26-27)

This verse has three keywords: purpose, discipline, and training. Only God knows your intention, but as you spend time with Him, He starts to reveal little by little the pieces of you that He requires for your purpose. Discipline is necessary, as it will keep you obedient, accountable, focused, driven, determined, faithful, and hopeful. The training may be a little difficult for some, as it will require work (mentally and physically, which can be draining), but what does not require work? Your heart is what will drive you to the next level of training. To get further in the race (journey), our spiritual self is what we want to train to be healthier, more focused, at peace, content, loved, educated, in God's word, and overflowing.

Restoration from Anything

Then if my people who are called by my name will humble themselves and pray and seek my face and turn from their wicked ways, I will hear from heaven and will forgive their sins and restore their land. (2 Chronicles 7:14)

To get restoration from anything that holds you down, here are the steps for us: BE HUMBLE - put everything you think you are to the side and be who He created you to be. PRAY - this is hard in moments of desperation, but I think our weakest moment is precisely when the next level of prayer needs to happen. He hears us even more; please understand, He is always by our side. SEEK - look for Him with all your heart. Run as fast as you can. Search the way we search for worldly things. To be in His presence takes time as well, just like anything else. TURN FROM WICKED WAYS - turn away from what hinders your walk with God, which will be hard at first, but the outcome of walking with Jesus is eternal and brings fulfillment to the heart. Nothing can compare to it. What can be more important than the Prince of Peace?

February 27

Be Dynamic

The Spirit alone gives eternal life. Human effort accomplishes nothing. And the very words I have spoken to you are spirit and life. (John 6:63)

Can our journey be more than what we make it? Yes, we are busy doing what we need to do daily. We are always running around with pages of to-do lists. Okay, here it goes: flip it and start following God's to-do list instead so you can handle your current tasks better, your stress decreases, and anxiousness or even fear drops. How do you start? Lean into Jesus with a dynamic (energetic, spirited, positive, practical, bold, and strong) attitude, believing that anything the enemy throws at you will crumble because you are so in the Spirit that nothing can harm you or frazzle your heart. Prayer should be on the list, as well as reading the Bible, so you can hear what He is saying. Just like the verse says, spoken words are from the Spirit and give life. Also, remember to be still in His presence as the enemy tries to steal your peace. Remember, our purpose is to do His will, not ours. Be the best you with a DYNAMIC attitude.

Be Weary but Keep Going with Jesus's Strength

Think of all the hostility he endured from sinful people; then you won't become weary and give up. (Hebrews 12:3)

There may be times you cannot go any further because our bodies can only take so much. Our body says quit, but our heart and mind say keep going. There is no giving up, and sometimes we are so mentally drained that those tears come out. But at that point, when we call on Him, we are rejuvenated. In this verse, we see we cannot quit. He endured so much for us: He never gives up on us, never leaves, and loves unconditionally. Thank Him for that, as we know it can be hard to love us sometimes. When I look at that cross, it is not hard to get back up, to know some of those stripes on His body had my name (my sins) on them. To know even with that done for us, He calls us to bring others. My challenge to you is that you give Him your time each day–even if it is silence, it is you and Him–the weariness will fall off you.

Purpose is to Share

But my life is worth nothing to me unless I use it for finishing the work assigned me by the Lord Jesus - the work of telling others the Good News about the wonderful grace of God. (Acts 20:24)

Like Jesus, we must do the assignment that God has placed in our hands: to spread the words of Jesus. We are to help those who are hopeless and encourage them when they cannot see the light in front of them due to the bondages that have blinded them. Paul suffered much and knew he had to do what he had to do to finish telling others about Jesus, even as he suffered. When we suffer, we desire to keep going because God must get the glory. Our suffering will never compare to Jesus. In all we do, He gets the credit always. As He increases in us, we should be decreasing. God will show you how your uniqueness will fulfill His purpose.

Following with a Cost

"But don't begin until you count the cost. For who would begin construction of a building without first calculating the cost to see if there is enough money to finish it? (Luke 14:28)

Jesus said it: do not begin until you count the cost. Can it be that is why so many people struggle with the back and forth, trying to make compromises with the world, confused (which, let us note, God, is not confusion) on what is right or wrong? He wants you to live and love but also to make sure that you are all in. Because if you are in, remember that it is not an easy path. If you are only halfway in, prepare yourself because it will be more difficult. He gave us this advice to make sure we knew what to expect upfront; may we remember this: "I must carry my cross, endure it, and keep following without complaining because it is part of my story on this journey toward Him and for His glory." Give everything to Him to be healed, restored, released, forgiven, for chains to fall off, or else our hearts will always be chasing something other than the only thing it should pursue: JESUS.

Wisdom from Heaven

I also pray that you will understand the incredible greatness of God's power for us who believe him. This is the same mighty power that raised Christ from the dead and seated him in the place of honor at God's right hand in the heavenly realms. (Ephesians 1:19-20)

The enemy can attack your identity to make you believe things that are not true of yourself because if he can get you to think that he has accomplished his goal. God is not a liar. Why do I say that? Because when He says you are loved, you are. When He says do not fear or doubt yourselves, then do not. I get it, we all fall into this type of thinking, but we will learn not to let our weaknesses get the best of us through His wisdom. The key is growing in knowing who He says you are and genuinely getting to know Jesus. I mean, study His words, hold them close to your heart, and hear Him because if you listen to Him, you will see when the enemy is trying to deceive you with his whispers. Please do not be ashamed of your weaknesses but be encouraged by them. Acknowledge your shortcomings by owning them. We will find freedom from their hold on us because it lets God know we need Him to gain strength or healing. He knows.

March 3

Wholeheartedly His

I was forty years old when Moses, the servant of the LORD, sent me from Kadesh-barnea to explore the land of Canaan. I returned and gave an honest report, but my brothers who went with me frightened the people from entering the Promised Land. For my part, I wholeheartedly followed the LORD my God. (Joshua 14:7-8)

What does this mean? Serve Jesus with a sincere and committed heart. Sometimes we want to know our calling now. We all want to be happy and peaceful, with our lives in order, no risking anything because that might hurt. But a broken arrow (deep-rooted pain, anxiety, bitterness, confused identity) in your heart is what will hinder your walk. You cannot fully or wholeheartedly be focused if that arrow is embedded deep. Jesus will remove the discouraged mindsets and replace them with thoughts of "I am," "I will," "I can," "I'm capable," and "I will take the risk because Jesus loves me and is for me." We are all given the courage and boldness to do what He needs us to do. In this verse, it says, "for my part." Yes, do your part when others do not. No wasting time: He needs YOU. Draw near to Him, and He listens to you.

March 4

Fragile Clay Jars

And yet, O LORD, you are our Father. We are the clay, and you are the potter. We all are formed by your hand. (Isaiah 64:8)

When you think of this, the potter is spinning to form a specific shape or jar, so some created parts of the clay are tossed, not needed, and other details saved because they are necessary. What am I saying? Our hearts are like clay jars. God is shaping them while taking out whatever injures them. He wants what He puts in it to stick; the rest must go. He molds us. No one else does. When He creates the jar, it is perfection. He places a light shining in our hearts because that is the only way we survive. This light is His truth, love, hope. He shows us how to discern, protect our heart, and when to open it. This light shines out and will shine on others. There is a crack in our clay jar, but it is still intact enough not to break. The clay is perfect because the potter oversees it. As He designed, our hearts are being changed by Jesus, challenged, healed, and reprogrammed to show us the realities of ourselves.

Asking for Understanding

So God replied, "Because you have asked for wisdom in governing my people with justice and have not asked for a long life or wealth or the death of your enemies—I will give you what you asked for! I will give you a wise and understanding heart such as no one else has had or ever will have! (1 Kings 3:11-12)

God is always ready to give us what we ask. But be prepared because He will respond by giving you more if your request is not a selfish one. Solomon asked for a wise and understanding heart (a heart that feels, hears, is fair, can discern good from bad, and loves with compassion and wants to do good) so that he can lead God's people. Why? Because only the Creator can give us the answer to how to teach the ones, He created. God granted his request and added that only He would have this specific wisdom, riches, fame, and long life. What does that mean? We all have a calling that is unique to each of us. Go for what God has called you to. Do not lose heart from what you have said or cannot change. Go forward and toward God with humbleness to help you. Ask God to change your heart to align with His, alter your selfishness to selflessness, unforgiveness to forgiveness, and your hardened heart to pure heart.

Awaken by Jesus

Go back to what you heard and believed at first; hold to it firmly. Repent and turn to me again. If you don't wake up, I will come to you suddenly, as unexpected as a thief. (Revelation 3:3)

To "awaken" means to rouse - a feeling to draw, call forth, bring out, or bring into being. When we first got saved, that "awaken" moment captured us. So, what happened? Why do we let it go so quickly when it took so much for us to find Him finally? Is it because we think it is okay to put Him on the sidelines and only call when we need something? What if He put us on the sidelines? God can do miracles if we genuinely believe. He does have requirements: things must go if they do not honor Him. It says, "go back to what you...believed at first" and "hold firmly" (like a football, do not drop it, pass it, or let it fumble), "repent and turn" back to God, or He will "come to us." Are we looking alive physically, but our hearts are dead to the things of God? If God is not in our hearts, how can we feel alive?

March 7

Need to Know

If you need wisdom, ask our generous God, and he will give it to you. He will not rebuke you for asking. (James 1:5)

What are you scared to ask God? Have you asked God what to do in your current situation? If the answer is to wait, then patiently wait without question. It is so simple yet challenging. He is the only One with answers. But remember, when you ask, make sure your faith in Him is in the right place. We cannot serve God and the world. It is that simple and true: if you do, you will have confusion because to follow God, our steps will be in order. He answers; when we do not know how to take steps forward or fear the change will cost us something. He knows that struggle within, but we cannot stay like that if we want to grow. I pray God removes those chains that hold you down. Ask Him to show and guide you so you can be unshakable, unstoppable, FREE, have loyalty only to Him, and not be torn between Him and the world. Be challenged to go to the next level with Him.

Working-Desire-Power

Dear friends, you always followed my instructions when I was with you. And now that I am away, it is even more important. Work hard to show the results of your salvation, obeying God with deep reverence and fear. For God is working in you, giving you the desire and the power to do what pleases him. (Philippians 2:12-13)

What a good reminder that we should not forget the day we got saved. Can I be honest? We sometimes do fail, especially during stumbling times. No worries - if you have, hold it deep in your hearts today because that is what keeps it honest with God and helps Him to continue working in your lives. He puts desires and the willpower to keep going where He is taking you. He knows the real you, no judgment. If no change after salvation, please let God do what He does best. Our behaviors must show a difference because He was not born for no reason and died for nothing. Be willing to change, get to your post, and keep going toward Him. He is worth it. He has shown me there is nothing impossible for Him to do or take care of, but I had to be obedient in prayer, have faith, and patiently wait to understand (yes, with tears sometimes). I hope you experience this as well.

Share in the Midst

Though I am surrounded by troubles, you will protect me from the anger of my enemies. You reach out your hand, and the power of your right hand saves me. (Psalm 138:7)

Something about Jesus keeps us going. Why do some of us care for the souls of others, whether they will go to heaven or hell? We must understand He expects us daily to share Him when He positions us in those moments, do we? It will not be easy to want to talk about anything during our storms, but I do not want to know that someone that Jesus sent my way never got to hear who He was, what He offers, and how He takes care of those who follow Him. If He protects us in our storms and from enemies, why would we stop spreading Him? It actually should increase because it is in the middle of our storms that we should magnify Him more, share His promises to help us keep moving and to help others seeking. Do not miss out on opportunities in sharing Him with people seeking because you do not want that in your heart or mind that maybe you could have made a difference. May God always give us a chance.

Cannot Stop His Words

And because I preach this Good News, I am suffering and have been chained like a criminal. But the word of God cannot be chained. (2 Timothy 2:9)

Being a follower (soldier) of Jesus is not an easy task. God has a plan to be accomplished, which is to give others hope that Jesus is the only way. He has chosen us to help. Some do not know Him–not by choice, maybe no one took the time to share about Him, or they have not had an encounter with someone who He has transformed. It is essential to understand that as soldiers of Jesus, we have a mission. That means to listen to the only One who gives commands and follows through with them. The obstacles that come your way may try to distract you from accomplishing this, but we must stand firm in love, in faith, in endurance, and prayer. As I read, His words, "cannot be chained," or, should I say, are UNSTOPPABLE. May He continue training and guiding us to lead others to Him, and may we never forget that He gets all the glory.

March 11

Hurricane

He spoke, and the winds rose, stirring up the waves. (Psalm 107:25)

When He spoke, the current moved the waves. It is a divine moment when He does speak. Yes, even when it is about a mistake we made. But God says because He loves. Today's title is "Hurricane" because it is a storm with a violent wind, so strong, fierce, and in control at that moment. Be that storm; do not be consumed by one. Hurricanes can be hardships, negative emotions, overthinking, brokenness by others, spiritual need and fleshly need at war inside. Here it goes: Humble (be this), Unshakable (yes, no matter what), Remove (obstacles), Restore (get back to Him), Identity (know you are His), Continue (in prayer), Always (pursue Him), Never (give up), Everlasting (the love He gives). Only One controls our storms and makes us peaceful inside.

March 12

I Agree

"The purpose of my covenant with the Levites was to bring life and peace, and that is what I gave them. This required reverence from them, and they greatly revered me and stood in awe of my name. (Malachi 2:5)

God is straightforward when He says: the same covenant that He made with the Levites should be our goal as well. He came to bring life and peace. Here it goes: make a covenant with Him now. Make it personal to yourselves: "Me and You, God. Your will, not mine, unless it aligns with You. Remove anything that hinders our relationship, help me to give up anything or anybody that distracts my attention, even if it is hard to strip away. You forgive in our covenant. Walking with You will allow us to lead others and help save souls that desperately search for hope. Sin is worth leaving behind when we have You, but we know that letting go is hard as we have lived with it for such a long time. Only You can overthrow it within us. Some may break their covenant but not I, for You are always with me, for me, and never against me. God, you are easy to love and hard to let go of." Like, I said, make it personal. What would you say in your covenant with Him?

I Am Here

"I also tell you this: If two of you agree here on earth concerning anything you ask, my Father in heaven will do it for you. For where two or three gather together as my followers, I am there among them."
(Matthew 18:19-20)

"Lord Jesus, thank You for your scripture that you are there when we gather as your followers." We must be His followers for Him to be amongst us, but also, please make sure when you get advice that it is from someone who has wisdom and will guide you to God's word. You will take a risk if the person you receive advice from is not following God. Who will lead you in the right direction? Be careful of the one that is going in circles, not getting anywhere. God is moving and changing hearts. Be obedient; wait for Him to say, "Now go for it." Know this journey can be lonely sometimes, but that is okay. Jesus walks with you when all else fails. Be tenacious with God, family, and friends. Please do not give up, and do not worry about what others think: it is your journey.

Bondages Within

Create in me a clean heart, O God. Renew a loyal spirit within me. (Psalm 51:10)

Bondages within will have some good memories, but they also contain reminders of what we made it through and show us God was there all along. He wants a broken, authentic, and repentant heart to restore. So, what am I saying? Let God clean every guilt, burden, stress, anxiety, fear, and resentment. Remove any barriers and replace them with His Spirit that calms the storms within. If you are lost, hold on. He will help you find your way again. Just like that, He will restore your broken heart to be stronger than ever and give you a spirit that will not allow the bondages to attach as it did before because this time, you are walking with Him within you.

Free from Perfect

Therefore, accept each other just as Christ has accepted you so that God will be given glory. (Romans 15:7)

Everyone wants to be accepted, but at what cost? Are we trying to be that perfect person for someone else? Here it goes being the best you God created does not mean being insensitive: we all have areas that God is working on to help us see others through His eyes. If you want to be accepted and fit in, know your boundaries for how far you will extend your heart. God takes you and me the way we are–however guarded, sensitive, introverted, extroverted, book smart, or street smart–that is the bottom line. "Lord Jesus, may we choose to be humble, gentle with others, patient, accepting (unconditional love), and unified. We need each other, and we need You. Amen."

Believe, Receive, Move

For I know the plans I have for you," says the LORD. "They are plans for good and not for disaster, to give you a future and a hope. In those days when you pray, I will listen. If you look for me wholeheartedly, you will find me. I will be found by you," says the LORD. "I will end your captivity and restore your fortunes. I will gather you out of the nations where I sent you and will bring you home again to your own land." (Jeremiah 29:11-14)

Why is it hard to do what the title says?

We are enough because our God says so in verse above. He has plans for us, for our good, for a future of HOPE. Pray, pray, pray - I cannot stress this enough because you will hear Him and receive guidance once in His presence. Our journey will be a lonely one sometimes. It is okay; not everyone gets us. Are you stuck at this moment? Are you lost? He is waiting to give you that confidence to run or walk that narrow path as the pillars of struggles fall along the way. Keep moving because, in the end, He is the one who gives you what you need to continue with boldness, courage, and an unstoppable heart.

The Great Guard

God is our refuge and strength, always ready to help in times of trouble. (Psalm 46:1)

"Pick us, Jesus, to guard." Sometimes we may not realize that the One we walk with has the power to overturn our situations. Yes, we need patience, faith, as well as trust. He guards the way before us: He covers, defends, watches over us, shields us, walks before us before we even get to that situation that will trip us if we are not in prayer. We hear Him say, "Not this way. Go to the right. Be careful with this person." He protects us against being damaged in all areas–emotional, mental, physical–but we must be obedient, not prideful. He does this for all who seek Him in this knowledge and understanding. It is available to all who believe that He is who He is and will do what He promised. The reward is wisdom and unfailing love. He is our PROMISE KEEPER.

Obedience at What Cost

Mary responded, "I am the Lord's servant. May everything you have said about me come true." And then the angel left her. (Luke 1:38)

What is obedience? It is to submit to another's authority. Mary, Jesus's mother, was obedient to God's plan. She had faith in Him and trusted Him even with the cost of what others said, or the embarrassment of assumptions. It did not matter because she was going to carry the One who would save the world. God chose her because He knew her faithful and obedient heart. God offers us the same thing. He may choose you to accomplish a task: trust Him and do it, even if it does not make sense, even if you get criticized, even if you walk alone because with your obedience and faithful walk will come with blessings, He has for you and your family. With what Jesus did for us, how can't we ask, "What can I do for you, Jesus?"

Will You Walk on Water?

Then Peter called to him, "Lord, if it's really you, tell me to come to you, walking on the water." (Matthew 14:28)

When Peter came out of the boat, as soon as he saw Jesus, he reacted immediately. He probably did not think about the storm, the others in the boat behind him or of drowning. Are we like that? Do we step out in faith? We may allow ourselves to lose focus, but with Jesus, we will stay focused. We are flawless; we are in His divine presence, He will, and He does control the storms of our lives. He is the Creator in control of all His creation. But our eyes cannot leave Him. We need to stay focused even if the storms hit our faces causing us to lose sight of Jesus. The enemy is desperate to try even at that moment to instill fears, anxiety, and doubt–that "I can't" mindset–but hold on to the truth (Jesus) who assures us, "I'm here; no need to fear."

Diligence

Good planning and hard work lead to prosperity, but hasty shortcuts lead to poverty. (Proverbs 21:5)

The word "diligence" means to be careful and persistent at work or putting forth effort. Yes, sharing the stories of Jesus can be challenging, especially when you try to help those who have been let down so often by the people they loved the most. The definition says it all: be careful. We always need to be careful wherever we go; as we know where we go, the enemy will always try to trip us up. But that is okay because you are walking with your armor. So, he can watch us win another for Jesus, but remember it is a process, requires work, effort, and compassion. We need to have a heart for others on different levels than us. The reason I say this is because some may struggle daily but encourage them to keep going. Struggle, endure and stand firm as best as you can on the foundation of Jesus.

Never Give Up on Loving

Love never gives up, never loses faith, is always hopeful, and endures through every circumstance. (1 Corinthians 13:7)

Jesus is the model for how to love uncon-ditionally. May He be the one you follow to guide all your relationships. It is needed to let the ones we love know how much they mean to us, but if they know your heart, they already know. So, say it to everyone who makes you realize you are loved, beautiful, strong, needed, that you matter in this world, that you count, that only you take that space in someone's heart because of your smile, generous spirit, or your presence in the room. "Lord Jesus, I pray that you send down extra love to show us how much we matter to You. Move our hearts, not to feel pressured, and help us walk daily with You: to show and share love, to give gifts, to say "I love you" without expectations so that it is genuine from the heart. Amen."

Next Steps

"I am leaving you with a gift—peace of mind and heart. And the peace I give is a gift the world cannot give. So don't be troubled or afraid. (John 14:27)

Go for it. What does that mean? Do what you are scared of doing. Do not let the enemy continue to have control over you. God is before you, so go to the next level in your journey. Thinking you are not good enough can sometimes cause confusion. Do not get lost in the thoughts that you do not pray like others; you do not know scripture; you do not know where to start. FLIP IT today: pray for boldness like never before; pray for the ones going beside you. The point is not to be stagnant. No more just being. So much is being offered by God, especially peace of mind, heart, and soul. Invest in people that you know are true, that care about your next level. Do not waste so much time on the ones who drain you. I am not saying break away from them; I am saying pray for them, but do not let it cling to your spirit so much that you miss out on what God has for you. God expects His creation to do so much more. Grab it, take steps toward it, pray, study, love, and have FAITH.

March 23

When Chosen

But Moses pleaded with the LORD, "O Lord, I'm not very good with words. I never have been, and I'm not now, even though you have spoken to me. I get tongue-tied, and my words get tangled." (Exodus 4:10)

God chose Moses, but Moses questioned his ability to speak. He felt that his words would sometimes be confusing when he talked to the people, tangled, not clear - yes, he had a speech impediment. But God will use who He wants; what is difficult for man is not for God. What am I saying? We must see beyond our weaknesses and see His greatness in us. Believe it, hold it tight, and most importantly, do not let go. We are to be who He calls us to be, plain and simple. Accept Him and let go of your old self–no grey areas–and unconditionally love everyone. Release those who hurt you, so as you do His will, your heart is right. Do not let your perception of weaknesses stop you, and if it does stop you, it is okay. God will continue doing His will but may add a little help to encourage you along the way.

March 24

I Just do not Understand

Jesus replied, "You don't understand now what I am doing, but someday you will." (John 13:7)

We can all relate to this, especially in challenging moments, but the beauty of it is that God is always on time if we are in tune with Him to see it. We can be in moments of confusion, but we cause that because He is not a confused God. But God is holy and in order, but when we let our heart take over, focusing on what we want versus what is right or what God wants, this is how we get confused. The intensity of letting God take over this confusion will knock you down because it takes out all that is confused in your mind and puts it in the correct fragments that we need to understand what He wants to do in our lives. We must trust without questioning or doubting when people are no longer part of our lives. It must happen because if they are not building or pouring good into you, how can you grow in your walk? So, He cleans the house. Yes, it hurts, but in time we look back and will understand. He knows best.

Divine Within

The LORD of Heaven's Armies has sworn this oath: "It will all happen as I have planned. It will be as I have decided. (Isaiah 14:24)

God has a plan, and He follows through, but specific steps will need to be in place to accomplish this. What do I mean? It will require surrendering, understanding that Jesus is in control, helpless sometimes, being at the edge of self because we cannot figure it out on our own. We must experience that moment within us when He captures our heart (like being saved), but I am saying that this moment should be a daily moment. Moments keep us in tune, in love, and obedient to God. Sometimes we forget. It never leaves; we just somehow let the divine moment go. That is why we are saved but not filled with the same overflowing love we once had. Get it back, get overflowed again, do not stay stagnant. Go for your purpose in this world, more divine moments, unconditional love, and opportunities to love and lead others to Jesus. If you do not do it, then what does this journey mean to you?

Breaking Walls to Rebuild Hearts

When I heard this, I sat down and wept. In fact, for days I mourned, fasted, and prayed to the God of heaven. (Nehemiah 1:4)

Nehemiah knew who to go to when the destruction of the walls happened: to the One he trusted, to the One who has promises for us. He was faithful and, at this moment, was advocating for those who probably did not know how to because they did not have the same relationship with God to go to Him. What is the point? When something knocks your walls down for a moment, we must go to God for answers. If we need to wait, we wait, but wouldn't we prefer to stay under His wings than any other who does not have our well-being in mind? Yes, broken walls are like broken hearts: it hurts, and we are vulnerable, exposing sensitivities that we do not want to show. How can God help, restore, or heal if he does not break down those walls or even put a crack in them just to let that heart breathe a little bit? "Lord Jesus, break down our walls, and send someone to help if needed so that healing happens. Amen."

March 27

The Humble Will See

The humble will see their God at work and be glad. Let all who seek God's help be encouraged. (Psalm 69:32)

A humble person is not proud and does not believe that they are better than others. We need to be humble, just like Jesus. We must be grounded in the Word and always fill our spirits to try our best to be this person. We must be focused and remember who we are. A humble person will surrender everything on their plate to Jesus, trust during times of unfairness, will know how to react when offended. Wisdom knows the battles fought and when to love others. Jesus wants us to humble ourselves, make things right, and keep moving toward Him. Let no one cause you to stumble when you aim to be HUMBLE, seeking to learn from others, at peace with yourself, and running closer to Jesus.

Unbreakable Bond

But if I tell him, 'Go farther—the arrows are still ahead of you,' then it will mean that you must leave immediately, for the LORD is sending you away. And may the LORD make us keep our promises to each other, for he has witnessed them." (1 Samuel 20:22-23)

True friendship should have God at the center. He represents all the characteristics needed in friendship, such as unconditional love, trust, honesty, loyalty, proximity, and presence in moments you need to be still or cry out. He can even be funny in certain situations. There is a story of King David and Jonathan, who had a bond that could have broken because Jonathan's father (Saul) wanted to kill David. This vow of love in their friendship and loyalty before God was important to them. They said goodbye with tears, but they were loyal forever. What am I saying? When God is in your friendship, it will survive. That is so that we know when to keep promises to each other or when not to. Love has to be unconditional, so it never fades. Their friendship was an example of this. Thank God for genuine friendships.

Soar Above Like an Eagle

But those who trust in the LORD will find new strength. They will soar high on wings like eagles. They will run and not grow weary. They will walk and not faint. (Isaiah 40:31)

An Eagle flies higher than any other bird. It represents freedom and courageous steps to look ahead during turbulent times. Those moments that rock you sideways or front and back are the moments to let God encourage your heart to look up and fly in the Eagle zone. As you are going through or around clouds that try to disturb your vision, keep going with all your will, strength, heart, power, determination, and fearless attitude. Then you get to the level of peace in your mind, heart, and soul with Jesus–until another turbulent situation. No looking down or around, only straight up with your armor tight, as things hit you but will not break you. Make that decision; no matter what, we will not give in to negative thoughts or give up on soaring into the arms of Jesus. It does not matter what others think. It is about your peace to be able to handle this journey.

March 30

Be the Best Example

But you, Timothy, certainly know what I teach, and how I live, and what my purpose in life is. You know my faith, my patience, my love, and my endurance. You know how much persecution and suffering I have endured. You know all about how I was persecuted in Antioch, Iconium, and Lystra—but the Lord rescued me from all of it. Yes, and everyone who wants to live a godly life in Christ Jesus will suffer persecution. (2 Timothy 3:10-12)

God will always send others to us to walk with and share our wisdom. Paul encourages Timothy, and he reminds him of what he has seen in Paul's life, such as who Paul was, his purpose, what he has endured, and who rescued him each time. Others need to know who we are by the way we live, our actions, or thoughts –who controls it? It is all about God, not us. God is who drives us – sad some lose focus. Each of you should be proud of your faith but know you will not fit with the crowd and will experience rejection, laughed at, or criticized as Jesus was. But you will be the overcomer with peace inside that they lack and that the ones He sends our way, may they see the truth we share; how stronger we get in our faith as those endured moments passed. And how God lifts us up to keep spreading His Word with more heart and intensity, so it will pierce their hearts that they cannot wait to have the same inner feeling as we do.

March 31

Nothing but Prayer

Then I said, "O LORD, God of heaven, the great and awesome God who keeps his covenant of unfailing love with those who love him and obey his commands, listen to my prayer! Look down and see me praying night and day for your people Israel. I confess that we have sinned against you. Yes, even my own family and I have sinned! (Nehemiah 1:5-6)

How do we react to situations? We can cry, be angry, let fear take over the heart and mind. We may doubt how to fix the problem and desperately cry out, "God, I have done everything; tell me what I am missing?" I love Nehemiah because he felt the pain of the destruction of the walls of Jerusalem. Not just that, but of the lives of God's people, the hopelessness. We need to be like that - to feel it as God shows us. Now Nehemiah knew where to go: to the only One that can restore it all. I learned at a women's conference once that before God responds, He hears and sees. But He also knows who is really with Him and aligned with His will or who is just having Him tag along just if there is a need. It does not work like that. As we ask God for help, make sure we ask for forgiveness in areas we offended Him, and then ask for assistance in the areas of struggles in our lives. He is waiting for us. That is a promise.

April 1

Return to Him

This is what the Sovereign LORD, the Holy One of Israel, says: "Only in returning to me and resting in me will you be saved. In quietness and confidence is your strength. But you would have none of it. (Isaiah 30:15)

I know we can all testify to those moments we went ahead of God and fell into the sin we had no business chasing or touching, eventually getting entangled. The whole time, our gentle God watches patiently and waits for us to say, "Help me." Our God never barges in and forces Himself on us. He knocks. We are so lucky that He forgives us and says, "Come back to me; it's okay." Can anyone relate to this? If you know you belong to Jesus and have strayed, wondering why everything is so hard, then I say go back and let God lead you. He is waiting. Behind Him, you will find rest, protection, restoration, and most importantly, His love and grace.

Fervent Prayers

He prayed more fervently, and he was in such agony of spirit that his sweat fell to the ground like great drops of blood. (Luke 22:44)

Fervent is to have a passionate intensity, deeply felt, sincere, emotional, and spirited. Jesus prayed when He struggled with the human side of Himself. He knew what was going to happen, but He knew it had to happen. God's will, not ours, right? As Jesus understood, it is not easy sometimes, but we must trust and believe God has plans for each of us. Will it always make sense? Not in moments of brokenness, loss, and anxiety–when we are running spiritually empty, but that is when we pray fervently. When you get to this place, it lets God know that you are ready to surrender and let Him take over truly. For some, you are tired of constant battles, and your fervent prayer is, "God, don't let go." But our most important prayer is to remember and fulfill our mission to do God's will.

April 3

It is a Choice

I have chosen to be faithful; I have determined to live by your regulations. (Psalm 119:30)

Free will is what we want and what God gives. What is the problem when we use this free will to go against God's will and end up struggling or crying out for God to help with the mess we made? Can I be honest? God's will is the goal: it comes with a cost. Yes, He will remove things or people that may be hindering you from receiving what He is holding for each of you. It is not easy, but anyone who experiences pain will heal and learn a lesson from it. I want you to know God knows, though He was not the initiator of what each of us experienced. He heals us and speaks the words, "I'm sorry you were hurt. I am sorry someone made you believe who you are is not good enough. I am sorry you believe it was your fault, it was not. You are courageous, strong, an overcomer, special, and so much more." Be confident in yourselves but always lean on God because He has you.

Spoken Faith

But we continue to preach because we have the same kind of faith the psalmist had when he said, "I believed in God, so I spoke." (2 Corinthians 4:13)

Sharing is what we should be doing daily.

Share who God is to your families, friends, co-workers, or anyone you encounter. Why? People can be blinded to what is around them (they are distracted by jobs, money, busyness, others) and sadly missing out on moments meant to lift their spiritual walk and well-being. Believing God is having the assurance and peace of mind. Everyone wants this peace but attaining it will cost. Yes, the adjustment in your life will have to happen. Just let go and let God take the wheel. New life grows, renewed hearts, bondages overpowered, identities restored, and rejuvenated souls. What was once walking defeated now walks in the victory? What was once fearful now is courageous? What was once barely loved now loves with an unconditional heart?

April 5

Different than Others

"My thoughts are nothing like your thoughts," says the LORD. "And my ways are far beyond anything you could imagine. (Isaiah 55:8)

Never compare Jesus to any other human. He will not let us down as others do; that is not His character nor who He is. His behavior is not like others'. He loves unconditionally and is so gentle in mannerisms. When others attack our character (that piercing of the heart feeling when words have struck us down), I imagine Jesus may have felt this sadness daily. He sees the challenges we endure and desires nothing but good for us. He came to save, love, forgive and help us figure out this journey with Him– even during storms. Let us surrender our worries, wounds, and any wrong that we have done that we have not forgiven ourselves for so that we are free in heart and mind. So His love can then do what only He can do.

H.O.P.E. is from Him Alone

Let all that I am wait quietly before God, for my hope is in him. (Psalm 62:5)

What do I mean by this hope we get from Him?

Sometimes you must hold on to what you know and believe God has poured into your (H)eart:

** Unconditional love for others.
** Identity as His sons and daughters.
** Discernment of who is for you.

Be (O)bedient all of the time–it is okay if things are not okay sometimes; endure and pray but do not stay down. Remember that you have (P)urpose: you do not need to know every detail; trust. Finally, have (E)xpectation for all He has for you: His promises, love, presence, and grace even in your disobedience. That is true friendship: never leaving. "Lord, may we surrender our hearts to You. Share Your peace and healing hands in whatever area that needs it. Fill us up with only what You can provide. And most importantly, thank You for choosing us and leading us daily. May we not forget the Fruit of the Spirit. Amen."

April 7

Right and True

For the word of the LORD holds true, and we can trust everything he does. (Psalm 33:4)

We reflect on the past during Easter, what we have overcome–some good and some bad. Not to discourage anyone but to show us that whatever Jesus says to us will always be correct and proper. Others may not offer that all the time, but He does. Jesus is faithful, comforting, honest, and our true best friend. When Jesus said, "It is finished" on the cross. His intention was for us to leave all our sins, regrets, disappointments, brokenness, our old selves, unforgiving hearts, and anything that separates us from God on the cross. Taking back anything from the cross can interfere with your relationship with Jesus and block all of the blessings He has for you.

Do Not Let Go of Confidence

So let us come boldly to the throne of our gracious God. There we will receive his mercy, and we will find grace to help us when we need it most. (Hebrews 4:16)

We can accomplish anything if we do what this verse says and "draw near to the throne of grace." Draw near Him, who knows all our insecurities and pieces of our character that need to be adjusted (let us be honest, we unintentionally hurt others and get hurt by others). We need motivation from others but first, go to your Creator. He is your motivator. Yes, to draw near to Him, you need to move forward into His domain of righteousness with compassion for others, understanding that not everyone sees life as we do. Some run faster to Jesus because their confidence in Him makes them more assertive in their Godly identities. However, others may still be running in worldly identities, not holding firmly to what God says about their identity, which causes that confidence to fade away. Walk each bold step knowing God has you and you have Him.

April 9

Make Your Time Matter

And this world is fading away, along with everything that people crave. But anyone who does what pleases God will live forever. (1 John 2:17)

As soon as we understand that we are not from this world, we start our journey. The struggle for many is time management: running around tight schedules while trying to accommodate others as we overfill this time created for God. Okay, let me clarify: the running around we do in our lives is not bad if in that time Jesus is thought of, and we are using that time to share who He is. Are we sharing what the Holy Spirit is directing us to do and putting into practice the characteristics He has placed in us or tweaked in us (we all need to be tweaked to be who we are in Jesus) to make a difference? Are we willing to take the time to help someone on their journey? Are we intentional to see people who matter to us, or do we think we will do it when we "have time to get to it?" What if we do not have time and miss the opportunity to do what Jesus wants? Take time, invest in others, make a difference, and persist in love.

April 10

Standing on Promises

And now that you belong to Christ, you are the true children of Abraham. You are his heirs, and God's promise to Abraham belongs to you. (Galatians 3:29)

We can stand (be situated in a position) on many things in life, such as what others promise us, the capabilities that we feel help us survive this journey, or our expectations, which can be unrealistic sometimes. All of this can be on shaky ground if it is not under God's will or promises. We will fall, trip, or stumble if our stance is not firm with confidence, boldness, and strength–unmovable and unshakable in Jesus. I pray for those on shaky ground to stand without fear, to stand on God's promises–not just for us but also for our loved ones who are struggling with their identities and confused by the enemy. Stand for them and with them until they can on their own, wearing those worn-out shoes that show the other battles we have walked through and won.

April 11

You Have Potential

We now have this light shining in our hearts, but we ourselves are like fragile clay jars containing this great treasure. This makes it clear that our great power is from God, not from ourselves. (2 Corinthians 4:7)

Potential is having or showing the capacity to become or develop into something in the future. Who do you think does not want that to come out of you? Yes, our enemy. God created us to do His will with the full potential that is within each of us, but we each must find it or want it as well. Some may know what that potential is, but it may mean a cost of self in many areas or letting go of people who are in the way, not supporting but discouraging you from developing it. Grab that potential because God will lead you, encourage you, and plant fire in you that no one can touch or extinguish. We need Him, so–yes– stay in the Word, pray, stop and be in His presence, then listen. Many in the Bible achieved their potential (this great power, poured into them by God) once they understood, were faithful, obedient, and willing to take that first step.

Sealed by God

Every word of God proves true. He is a shield to all who come to him for protection. Do not add to his words, or he may rebuke you and expose you as a liar. (Proverbs 30:5-6)

This verse says every word of God is truth. Let us think about this: So, what He promises, He will do? Yes. He will not leave us, even in our most challenging moments? No, He will not. Will He protect us from our enemies? Yes. To be saved by His covering, we need to find, seek, or run to Him. Not doing so is not an option in our Christian journey. It also says we are not to add to His words. Hmm, has anyone ever done that? We must be careful because, as you read, it also says He will rebuke us. His words heal, but sometimes we feel that His words break us. However, He sometimes must break us to restore us when we are lost, for we are His.

Find Your Platform

The king took his place of authority beside the pillar and renewed the covenant in the LORD's presence. He pledged to obey the LORD by keeping all his commands, laws, and decrees with all his heart and soul. In this way, he confirmed all the terms of the covenant that were written in the scroll, and all the people pledged themselves to the covenant. (2 Kings 23:3)

To find your platform means to go to your next level and identify your plan of action. According to this verse, King Josiah reigned for 31 years. He was a righteous king that took his platform when he found out that his ancestors did not follow the covenant made with God, and now his people would suffer the consequences. God is the one who raises you, and this is important because you will lead others–not one left behind (Ohana) as you walk with honor, love, gratitude, and heart. As the king did, we must give all our heart and soul to our covenant with God because we need to feel it that deep. Find your platform, and when you find it, stand firm. He sees you, and you will find peace in His presence as you stand.

April 14

Make It Personal

Don't be afraid, for I am with you. Don't be discouraged, for I am your God. I will strengthen you and help you. I will hold you up with my victorious right hand. (Isaiah 41:10)

When we read a verse, add your name. It makes you feel that He is talking directly to you. Now let me make it clear: whether you add your name or not, God is listening. Here is an example: "So don't worry, (add your name). Do not be afraid (add your name). I will make you strong (add your name). And I will help you and support you, (add your name), with my right hand that saves you." It comforts, strengthens, and validates, even more, His existence. It connects us in closeness with Jesus as He assures us that we are okay, that He has us, and knows the obstacles set before us. But also, healing is taking place. As we lay out all our concerns, we must remember that God provides all we need to press on.

April 15

What Does It Take to Get it?

That is why I use these parables, For they look, but they don't really see. They hear, but they don't really listen or understand. (Matthew 13:13)

The Bible says we must listen to God to gain understanding and knowledge. It makes a big difference. The best way to do it is to pour into the Bible with anticipation. You will learn the character of God; I pray you never forget who you are–all layers. There are people with a wall so thick that they do not allow God and others to be in their lives. They do not see the good in these people or hear the good about them from God, who has poured into them to deliver what they need. Sometimes we miss His message because we cannot see or hear the truth due to worldly entertainment. Having limited understanding is okay, but we need His truth to be strong and effective in our minds so that we do see God working and hear His gentle whispers of direction. It can be an obstacle because of that lack of knowledge. Run, seek wisdom, and be encouraged as you find it.

April 16

Just a Carpenter

Then they scoffed, "He's just a carpenter, the son of Mary and the brother of James, Joseph, Judas, and Simon. And his sisters live right here among us." They were deeply offended and refused to believe in him. (Mark 6:3)

Who would have known but Mother Mary that this carpenter would be our Savior? A carpenter is detailed, communicative, physically strong, technically skilled, and mathematical–that is who our Savior is. But now, let us apply these traits to how Jesus interacts with us. The Bible says we are wonderfully made (this covers the unique details placed inside of us). He communicates with us using the Holy Spirit. He makes us strong in His presence. The Spirit is controlling and directing our critical thinking. He uses His technical skills with tools, such as prayer, scripture, church, and community groups. When needed, His mathematics will configure our hearts to be in the correct measurements required to be at a place of healing. God will cut out what is no longer needed or what is hindering you, and He will shape you into what He wants you to be by installing new things in you.

April 17

Hated for Loving

"If the world hates you, remember that it hated me first. (John 15:18)

As soon as we said yes to Jesus, we knew that the enemy would always throw arrows at us. So, what do we do? Yes, keep growing in faith and praying for the spiritually blinded ones who cannot see who Jesus is because pride, lack of knowledge, worldly interest, and sin gets in the way. But we need to understand this and be sensitive to it. People may fear or doubt the unknown. It can be uncomfortable, just like we were before we met Jesus. Not all hate us; some do not know how to take the first step into humility and in love toward Jesus. The best defense against those against us is PRAYER–not worrying or stressing about it–as our Father will take control over it. Some people did not like Jesus, so we must understand we will be in that position sometimes. He kept going through the crowds, praying, healing, and loving, so we need to do that the best we can.

We Will Be Blessed

Wherever you go and whatever you do, you will be blessed. (Deuteronomy 28:6)

This verse is encouraging, even when things get difficult while trying to be obedient and be that person God has created us to be. Who does not want the favor of God? But we need to sacrifice, change, seek, be encouraged, and ask for prayer when needed, as this journey was not to walk with others. Be still in those moments when it does not make sense because being obedient will require the discipline of not wavering to anyone if it is not right in your spirit and what the Word says. We do not follow; we lead. The Bible says we will experience blessings if we obey (so true - I know we all have felt touched when we have been fully obedient, and we see the difference when we are not). Keep pressing on—no giving up. And as we endure those arrows of difficulty, we stand firm on His promises and stay obedient through it all. It will be worth it because our God is a Promise Keeper.

April 19

Keep Prospering

They are like trees planted along the riverbank, bearing fruit each season. Their leaves never wither, and they prosper in all they do. (Psalm 1:3)

To prosper, you need something deep inside that makes you overflow with joy. Yes, that seed of faith in Jesus. You will always succeed if you stay in His presence, but it may not look the way you want it to look. It will be His will and His way. The word prosper means to succeed, flourish, and do well. It is excellent, thriving, and good for your well-being, it encourages, and it is a blessing. Hmm, it sounds like this journey–what it can be like when our focus is totally on Jesus, without distractions of the world. Here is my point: to prosper, you need Jesus. It is not like we can shop for what we want. It is what you must take without doubt or question, enduring the bad and holding on to the good. In whatever situation, you will walk away learning something about yourself.

April 20

Abide

Remain in me, and I will remain in you. For a branch cannot produce fruit if it is severed from the vine, and you cannot be fruitful unless you remain in me. (John 15:4)

There was a time when I was driving, and I was behind a car with a license plate that said, "ABIDE." It was at 5:56 AM. It was a reminder to me to remain in Jesus. But then the next day, it happened to me again–same place, same car–but I was behind it at 6:08 AM. How can that be? But God. We must remain in Him, and He will remain in us. I love that God will find a way to tell us that He knows where we are at, He sees our efforts and considers the running and pondering, but He knows who loves Him. So, remain in Him when you do not know. I know the questions I had at that moment, and He responded immediately. Abiding in Him is being committed to His ways, rules, and waiting on His answers. So yes, patience is needed. Just being quiet in His presence keeps you encouraged and allows you to feel His love. It is not that others do not love us, but there is something about God's love that overflows the heart so that you feel safe.

April 21

Indestructible Mustard Seed

"You don't have enough faith." Jesus told them. "I tell you the truth, if you had faith even as small as a mustard seed, you could say to this mountain, 'Move from here to there,' and it would move. Nothing would be impossible." (Matthew 17:20)

Indestructible means enduring forever, never dying, without end; this represents our faith, that nothing or nobody can break unless we allow it. But we must think about the sacrifice for us, the cost, the pain to capture the point. Sometimes there is a tug of war within that we feel when we need to make choices about what is right to do, but when we shift our perspective to remember the cross and what Jesus went through, we know what we need to do or who we need to choose. Today, choose Jesus's way. Choose peace in your situation. Choose unconditional love. Hold your mustard seed tight– that is what you must focus on in hard times and good times. It will make you stand assertively and bolder without anxious thoughts.

Which One is Leading Soul or Spirit?

For the word of God is alive and powerful. It is sharper than the sharpest two-edged sword, cutting between soul and spirit, between joint and marrow. It exposes our innermost thoughts and desires. (Hebrews 4:12)

We know if the Holy Spirit is leading, the focus is not on us. It is all about God and His plans, which we are to listen to and follow. Decisions will challenge us because the Spirit will not give peace if the decision is not correct or aligned with Him. Our emotions lead the soul, will, mind, or personality. The word of God is like a sword that will cut between our soul and spirit. Why? Because to serve God, we cannot be led by both, as one helps itself and the other will serve God, which is what we seek; this will capture the soul if we trust the Holy Spirit to take over. Some souls are lost and constantly seeking peace, serenity, or direction from the world, but they do not get far because what they seek is only what the Holy Spirit offers. Until that surrendering happens, they stay stagnant or lost. Seek, run, or jump, but make sure to find the Holy Spirit.

April 23

Change

And I will give you a new heart, and I will put a new spirit in you. I will take out your stony, stubborn heart and give you a tender, responsive heart. (Ezekiel 36:26)

Yes, only Jesus give us a new heart and spirit. Our flesh is weak; we struggle. May we remember that having a new soul comes with having a different view and putting Him in the driver seat through those roads of self-destruction that lead to bondages. May He give us the boldness to make healthy changes for our souls and help others figure this out. Remove those stones (brokenness, expectations, distorted views of ourselves, anxiety, depression) in our hearts. Do what releases those bondages one step at a time. It will help, refresh, restore, and motivate you to want more of God's presence because bondages hold you down and discourage you. But we always win with Jesus. Be strong, be you, and be ready.

Selfish Ways Must Go

He died for everyone so that those who receive his new life will no longer live for themselves. Instead, they will live for Christ, who died and was raised for them. (2 Corinthians 5:15)

This verse says once we accept Jesus, we should no longer live for ourselves. Why? Because how can we do His will when we are focus on "me" instead of the "we." It is not easy for us to make this adjustment, but we will not prosper if we do not let go of control, trusting God, and understanding that it is no longer about the individual needs. It is about what Jesus wants and needs for His purpose. We cannot have both the old life and the new life. Remember, no in-between or grey areas. The old life can be easy, as it is the norm. But can we find inner peace going back to that life after we found Jesus? No one can say there is a comparison. A new life with Jesus is the only way to inner peace, hope, love, contentment, trust, and faith. We no longer have a human perspective, but a Godly perspective is our new life. We sometimes forget, but it is okay. He knows.

April 25

Seeds on Rocky Soil

The seeds on the rocky soil represent those who hear the message and receive it with joy. But since they don't have deep roots, they believe for a while, then they fall away when they face temptation. (Luke 8:13)

The seed is (the word of God). If you love to plant, you know the soil has to be good , so what we plant will grow, but if a seed is on rocky soil, there will be weeds, rocks, sticks, or other things that will interrupt the growth. The word of God is not always received the way it should be by His creation, maybe because it convicts the hearts with truth. Still, how we hear His words can depend on how rooted we are in it (by reading, studying, applying, and praying) so that the world's temptations will not distract or steal us from Him. If not, it will cause sinking slowly in this rocky soil, yeah results in bondages, no peace, and confusion. We all have fallen. Get up and run to Him for forgiveness and get back on track without going backward. Forward is the only way.

April 26

Here We Are

"If only you would prepare your heart and lift up your hands to him in prayer! Get rid of your sins and leave all iniquity behind you. Then your face will brighten with innocence. You will be strong and free of fear. (Job 11:13-15)

Surrender, give up, and turn to Him is what the message is expressing. Something so simple, yet so hard to do. Why? Because it requires no longer having a hold on things or people. It is letting go of what or who we love and placing it at the hands of Jesus. It will leave us feeling vulnerable, unguarded, or no longer in charge. But flip it: let go of what can sometimes wear you down emotionally, mentally, or physically, and give it to Jesus, who is there to take it. Some think vulnerability is terrible; some may think it is weakness, failure, being too sensitive, or overly emotional, but it is honest about how God made us. So, stay focused on that, and be you inside and out. Give the rest to God.

Pour Out What Has Been Given to You

*"Listen, O Israel! The LORD is our God, the LORD alone.
(Deuteronomy 6:4)*

As you pour out what our Creator has poured in, others will be blessed, healed, and restored. It is not easy to do because resistance is there, but what is impossible for our God? God uses us, and His love pours out like a splash of rain and showers others. They do not understand this unconditional love. Why would someone want to share with me? But we need to be ready, willing, wanting, striving, hungering, and running to that table for His words, protection, love, guidance, patience, and heart. Your feelings will get hurt sometimes, or we will lose friendships, but we have an assignment to do that has to be a priority above all, people, and above ourselves. Created to multiply for Jesus is our purpose. That is the goal, as so many are hurting, seeking, waiting, and trying to find who they are.

Do You Belong to Him?

Anyone who belongs to God listens gladly to the words of God. But you don't listen because you don't belong to God." (John 8:47)

This verse says if we belong to God, we will listen to His words. But all of us have been at a point or are currently at the point where we do not listen because why would we want correction? Why listen when we are doing our will, and God's will only makes us uncomfortable? But we also know anything not associated with God will not work. We may have good times, but we will not be satisfied because of the void that has to be filled only by the presence of Jesus, not the world. Listening to His words is comforting, letting us know we are not alone. They give direction, educate us, correct us for our well-being, and they keep us strong. To be part of His team, we are either all in or all out–no middle. I pray for you to hear God's word, and anything that the enemy says to you will not shake you, break you or move you. Stand on all the words of Jesus, which are promises and true.

April 29

Heavenly Blessings

All praise to God, the Father of our Lord Jesus Christ, who has blessed us with every spiritual blessing in the heavenly realms because we are united with Christ. (Ephesians 1:3)

Heavenly blessings: two perfect words that we know are good. One refers to where our God sees us and where we will someday be: a place of no hardships, tears, brokenness, or pain but rather a place of joy, happiness, and unconditional love. The other is God's favor and protection upon us, and we get to experience every (not partial or half) spiritual blessing in Christ. Abide in Him alone, and these are the rewards, gifts, and promises for our obedience, trust, and faithfulness. Be hopeful always, especially when we cannot think or see straight. Know that we have a backup in heaven–our Father and our loved ones, who we never forget to keep in our hearts, who remind us we are strong and never to give up.

April 30

Strive on Water

God will push down Moab's people as a swimmer pushes down water with his hands. He will end their pride and all their evil works. (Isaiah 25:11)

To strive is to struggle or fight vigorously. I started to think of a swimmer: what it takes to stay above the water, how the person must use the whole body to remain above and prevent drowning–using arms, hands, feet–and how they must focus ahead. The verse says God will push down Moab's people, who were enemies of the Israelites, the way a swimmer pushes down water. What does He mean? Each stroke pulls you forward and pushes down water (those challenging issues in our lives or people that are distracting us), but what I like is that each stroke makes us stronger in faith, focused, and challenged to the best of our ability to see things or people that are for us or not. As we swim, we look left, right, and ahead, but never behind. We overcame any hardships that came our way to propel us to get to the next level. God cleared the waves (enemy tactics). We are on the ripple of the path ahead. Will you swim?

May 1

Keep

"Keep on asking, and you will receive what you ask for. Keep on seeking, and you will find. Keep on knocking, and the door will be opened to you. For everyone who asks, receives. Everyone who seeks, finds. And to everyone who knocks, the door will be opened. (Matthew 7:7-8)

To keep is to continue, not cease, go on, persist in, or carry on a task. The Bible says for effective prayer to keep asking and seeking. He will open the door if it is His will. Now let us think about this: it will be hard to ask and not receive right away, as I know that is how some of us are. Instead of getting anxious, burdened, troubled, confused, or, yes, even angry, why not just continue diving into the Bible and reading about how so many people waited, and then the blessings came? Somehow the amount of time that passed did not matter anymore or was forgotten. Stepping back in prayer is where He wants us. He is our tower that will not break. He is that person who carries us forward when our brains hurt so much from overthinking worst-case scenarios. Pray until it wears you down–NO stopping. We will unlock those doors to peace, trust, answers, and direction to the right path.

May 2

Rays of Peace

'May the LORD bless you and protect you. May the LORD smile on you and be gracious to you. May the LORD show you his favor and give you his peace.'
(Numbers 6:24-26)

I am not sure if anyone else does this, but I do. In my most challenging times, I look at the sky, and something about that causes me to be in awe of His peace. We know He walks with us, fills our cups, holds us, loves us, and forgives us. So, as we read, He turns His face toward us and gives us peace. Yes, it is like He knows we are trying. He does not want us to lose heart, so as He looks down at your situation, God is already working on the answer that He will direct you to find. It requires leaning on your faith that the God you love and honor will give you something to hold on to when you are at the edge. He encourages us as we look up and places this peace inside that carries us through to the next time we need to look up again. So, lookup. God has more than you can imagine.

May 3

Constantly Seeking

I took my troubles to the LORD; I cried out to him, and he answered my prayer. (Psalm 120:1)

We all want our prayers answered, espe-cially those in moments of seeking answers: not just during hardships, but in "I don't know" moments, too. The Bible says, *"Confess your sins to each other and pray for each other so that you may be healed. The earnest prayer of a righteous person has great power and produces wonderful results"* (James 5:16). Our prayers should be "earnest prayers," which means they should be sincere, serious, committed, deeply felt, wholehearted, and honest. We should believe it because prayer is going to Jesus, ready to help—seemingly desperate or straightforward times. We never lose with Him. Suppose you have not experienced answered powerful prayer. In that case, I pray that you do it soon, as it is the most fulfilling, overwhelming, and emotional moment because it validates that He hears you, sees you, and feels your heart, especially those prayers which no one knew but Him. While others may pray for you–which is excellent–He directly answers you. Wait, serve, and trust as He brings your answers that will align with His will. His peace is the sign that He has you.

May 4

Jesus or the World?

Her sister, Mary, sat at the Lord's feet, listening to what he taught. (Luke 10:39)

There is a story of two sisters, Mary and Martha. When Jesus shows up at their door, Mary stops everything and gives Him all the attention, but Martha does the opposite. She means well, but she is trying to put things in order in the house. He is essential to her, but He was not her focus at that moment. Here it goes: if Jesus is our focus, then we can handle life a little bit better. He is the core of our hearts. He controls the relationships in our lives, our jobs, our families, everywhere we go, and those we encounter–I think you get the picture. Instead, we make it about what we want. Is it Him or our selfish desires influenced by what the world expects? He wants us all happy, but even though He is the core of our hearts, some put Him away until Sunday. But they wonder why they are struggling Monday through Saturday. Are you Mary or Martha? Do not miss the opportunity to be in His presence when He shows up at your doorstep.

May 5

Revolving Door

Well then, should we keep on sinning so that God can show us more and more of his wonderful grace? Of course not! Since we have died to sin, how can we continue to live in it? (Romans 6:1-2)

Something must change if you feel you are always in the same situation or sin. It may be a different atmosphere, but it is a continuous cycle. Some may wonder why they are so tired, why they are stuck just like a revolving door. Sometimes that door gets jammed, and to get it moving, we need to push forward in the next direction. This same mindset we should have in life when it seems jammed. Is this just a moment God is reminding us to change direction? Push forward. You cannot go back to fix what caused you to get stuck. As you push forward, there will be a way out–to a new path on your journey, to new outlooks waiting for you to explore, to new people to meet and share Jesus, and to new challenges to experience. We need to let go of would have, should have, or could have. Stay humble, pray, seek, and turn away from what is not of God, and He will listen.

The Best for Him

Meanwhile, Jesus was in Bethany at the home of Simon, a man who had previously had leprosy. While he was eating, a woman came in with a beautiful alabaster jar of expensive perfume made from essence of nard. She broke open the jar and poured the perfume over his head. (Mark 14:3)

Jesus does the best for us daily and never withholds anything unless it will harm us or is not for us. I always remind my sisters that He is a gentle God. Do we give Him our best, or do we walk with this mentality of doing the minimum for Him because it is enough for us? We think, "This is what I need to get through, using this box of Jesus that I will occasionally open when I need help or when it's convenient for me." If you read the verse, it says she poured the costly perfume, not caring what others thought or that she looked foolish. Understand that to others, when we follow Jesus, we may look silly. I would rather be foolish and blessed than broken into pieces with no purpose. We need to pour out our best for the Creator as the woman in this verse did, as she knew He would not always be there in person. We, the creation, were born to serve Him but without boxed expectations. We will never lose with Him. Carry Him with you daily, in every moment. That is all we need.

He Has to be Enough

Each time he said, "My grace is all you need. My power works best in weakness." So now I am glad to boast about my weaknesses, so that the power of Christ can work through me. That is why I take pleasure in my weaknesses, and in the insults, hardships, persecutions, and troubles that I suffer for Christ. For when I am weak, then I am strong. (2 Corinthians 12:9-10)

Here it goes: when life hits you hard, He is who will pick you up when you do not want to move. He says, "GET UP. We still have to keep going." I understand that this is a part of carrying your cross, but you are not alone. He is the strength we need daily. We try to hide behind a mask, but if Jesus is not in the core of our hearts, I guarantee we will crumble and stumble. When you know who you are, it challenges you when the tough times come. The Spirit does not let you stay down because His peace carries you, but it only happens if you let the Holy Spirit take control. So yes, if you feel the need to always be in control, that must go out the window. In life with Jesus, He rules, authorizes, removes who or what is not for us, and pours out what is needed to continue in our journey. It is okay not to be okay, as my sister once told me. Do not stay in those emotions too long. Get back up. Jesus is all we need at any moment.

May 8

Are You Seen?

But the person who loves God is the one whom God recognizes. (1 Corinthians 8:3)

There is a difference between being loved by people and being loved by God. Let me clarify others can love us, but it will never compare to the love God gives each of us. Know that He created us with a void only He can fill. We surround ourselves with family and friends and still feel this void. To be recognized by God is to be seen for our hearts, identity, and loving Him so much that we do our best to do right, to be seen by how we love others the way He wants us to love (yes, even the ones who challenge our love). God knows who genuinely loves Him, who makes an effort to be recognized by Him: the ones who do not stop, go where He sends them, who give of themselves because they are faithful and obedient. God sees sacrifice, effort and hears the prayers of the righteous. To those He gives favor.

Privilege or Burden?

By God's grace and mighty power, I have been given the privilege of serving him by spreading this Good News. (Ephesians 3:7)

The word privilege means a special right or advantage granted only to a person or group. He chose us and has chosen others. Some will take the challenge of the journey, and some may not qualify for now. To serve Him, we need to have a mindset of "Here I am," not "Here I go away." God gives grace and power, and we get to serve Him. God saved us, so we should take every opportunity to help Him by sharing who He is. He places us in different places because there is a lot to cover in this world. That is our assignment. During the messiness of life, to know that at our worst, He took time to mend our hearts, we should be running to Him asking, "Where do you want me to go now?" Or "Who should I help, listen to, or hold today, God?" It is an honor to be chosen. I love spreading His love and truth, as I know you do too. Our God is an unshakable and unbreakable God who helps us get through each day. Serve Him today in whatever capacity you can.

See Beyond What is in Front of You

All who are victorious will inherit all these blessings, and I will be their God, and they will be my children. (Revelation 21:7)

We take different directions in our lives, and sometimes we cannot see where we are going because our views can be misleading. But God reminds us in this verse that "all who are victorious will inherit all the blessings." It is exciting to know that we can attain this if we keep going and look beyond. So those feelings of fear, stress, anxiety, and overloaded to-do lists do not have a hold on us or will not blind us to what God has for us. It is such an honor to be His children. No one knows each of us better than Him. He knows how to comfort us, discipline us, and understand us in good and challenging times. He is beyond enough. He is who He says He is, so please do not let anyone ever convince you otherwise. Get to know Him so you can see the picture of the God of possibilities.

Dedicate Your Life to go Where He Sends You

But if I live, I can do more fruitful work for Christ. So I really don't know which is better. (Philippians 1:22)

What do you want God to say of you? Did your actions bring Him honor, or did they tear Him down? Our purpose is to help others move toward Jesus. Suppose you failed in the past, no worries. Start today. God is a God of change if we make things right with Him. When we find that final puzzle piece to our identity, all we want to do is love others, serve, bless them, and give God all the glory because He changed the hearts not valued by others. We get an opportunity to share the perspective of God to some who still doubt Him because somewhere along their journey, they let others take His place, or life hardships hit so hard that they did not know what they should believe. Help those that need to get back on track. God is already there.

Red Sea Experience

So the people of Israel walked through the middle of the sea on dry ground, with walls of water on each side! (Exodus 14:22)

God divided the sea into two water walls so the Israelites can go through to the dry land on the other side as the Egyptians are chasing them. Fear and anxieties can appear, but it does not matter who is chasing us with God. He will control the consequences of going against Him or His people (on who will go through or who will drown). Apply this to our lives; our journey starts in one place: the dry land we leave then goes through the sea. The walls of water can represent our stories (childhood, adulthood, relationships, joyful moments, identity phases, career changes, brokenhearted moments, conflicts, or loss of loved ones – He never left us in all of this). We must pray, press forward, and believe God will get us through it all as we walk to the other side because guess what? He is waiting for YOU to take you to the next level of your faith.

Unstoppable Prayers

One day Jesus told his disciples a story to show that they should always pray and never give up. (Luke 18:1)

Prayer is the best way to connect to God and maintain a relationship with Him. If we pray effectively, wounds will get healed. Prayer breaks what we cannot humanly do. Its power is driven by believing that we can conquer any giants with our Lord. Do we believe it? If we do not, ask God to help those holding us back, keeping us from the blessings waiting for us to get to the next level. We cannot do anything without prayer—it is protection, love, security, safety; it says you are okay. Keep pressing forward; it is the best and only weapon to defeat the enemy's tactics to break you. Prayer is asking God to fight for you, so step back, watch and know God will move in His timing.

May 14

The Reason He Came

The thief's purpose is to steal and kill and destroy. My purpose is to give them a rich and satisfying life. (John 10:10)

Nothing else matters aside from Him–wherever you are at in your journey. Put it in perspective: He came to give us life. Do not walk around lifeless, but walk with boldness, confidence, and encouragement. He is victorious, so we are victorious. He loves, so we love. He forgives, so we forgive. He does not carry bondages, so try your best not to either. I can go on, but you get my point. I love that with God; we do not need to wear a mask as some people do. We can be who we are. So, with that, be you, His beloved daughter, the one who belongs wherever His presence is. Nothing else matters.

The Creator is Watching

You see, we are not like the many hucksters who preach for personal profit. We preach the word of God with sincerity and with Christ's authority, knowing that God is watching us. (2 Corinthians 2:17)

We are not to ever guess what God says in the Bible. Please make sure when you are sharing, it is what He said. Sincerity and Authority = Impact. They go hand and hand because as you speak from the heart of the wisdom you know; or tell your testimonies, those are vulnerable moments that happened, so how can you not be sincere (honest, truth, or straightforward). Being in this state of mind and heart is what Jesus wants because He is all this and more, and we as His saved children have the authority. I know it is hard to share Jesus's truth with others, but we have to; that is why we have power; it is part of who we are. We should love that He watches because He empowers, protects, and directs us to deliver His message as best as we can, so we impact lives forever. Yes, we may mess up the delivery of a message. Still, He corrects it with grace from others to show it is okay.

Take the Invitation

So we tell others about Christ, warning everyone and teaching everyone with all the wisdom God has given us. We want to present them to God, perfect in their relationship to Christ. (Colossians 1:28)

Visualize this: Jesus, God, and the Holy Spirit are at the table with an empty seat for each of us to sit. Please understand this invitation to the table. It means bringing everything to them, putting it in front of them to surrender, and trusting their guidance. Do not let anyone prevent you from getting your seat. It is yours. You come as you are. It has nothing to do with frequent sittings. He wants moments that are intimate and real. Sharing with Him is a step to help us go deeper. Through surrendering it, you start the process of healing with God. Our frequent trips to the table become just that: a sitting but not a cleansing if we do not. Recovery must happen to provide direction for where to go, what to do, and forgiveness. He knows and asks; do you love me? So why not be obedient in this area? Who is the judge of all? Our experiences will each be different but be at the table daily. It is a must.

May 17

Think like Jesus

You must have the same attitude that Christ Jesus had. (Philippians 2:5)

Stay humble to God. When you do, you can handle life better. There will be no issues that you cannot take. It is all about God–no matter what happens. When we fail, break, hurt, or feel defeated, God has it, will fix it, and restore it. But let us make sure we are doing our part with people–loving them, forgiving them, helping the ones in need, raising up and not tearing down those who will elevate (note: everybody will be at His time or when they open their eyes and see He is what they lack). Humbleness comes with a cost: walking alone (this can be hard) and losing people, but they did not hold on to see what God was doing in your life that would also bless them. It is okay: if you cannot be you, then it is not meant to be. God will send the ones you need. You will persist because He will overflow your mind with good. Enduring life is part of the journey; it makes you stronger. May God give us what we need to be humble and give us the heart to help those we know are lost. I want to lift everyone we know who is searching for salvation at this moment, that has not given up, is stuck, and does not know why. May we all have an opportunity to talk about Jesus, our

Hope, to the ones who feel hopeless. Be sensitive to the people you approach. Show your light today with a smile.

May 18

Accepting Consequence for Your Actions

For I recognize my rebellion; it haunts me day and night. Against you, and you alone, have I sinned; I have done what is evil in your sight. You will be proved right in what you say, and your judgment against me is just. (Psalm 51:3-4)

You hear it all the time: we are sinners. Yes, but what does that mean? Be proud of it? Is this assurance of being saved and knowing God forgives so we think we can do what we want? Jesus paid a high price for us, so why is it so hard for us? We have a gentle God who, when we break, allows us to figure it out until we realize that we cannot do it without Him. A life without Him (no grey areas) has no hope. We cannot survive, and so many think they will until reality hits and the void inside is left unfilled again. King David's sin gave him no peace–not only because of what he did but also because he sinned against the Prince of Peace. God deserves our apology. We must give Him all the guilt after asking for forgiveness. I pray we surrender what needs to go to the altar to find our identity in true worship. There is grace, growth in faith, and no going backward on our journeys.

Choose Your Battles

Take control of what I say, O LORD, and guard my lips. (Psalm 141:3)

When we want to argue a battle that we think needs to be won, we all have been there. The Bible says two things: 1) guard our mouths. Sometimes we need a filter, as words can hurt others if they misunderstand what we meant to say 2) for God to keep watch over our words. Yes, take control, Lord. We always somehow mess up. We need the Holy Spirit to remind us who we are because that will keep us in check, in our behaviors, and especially in our speech. That is why it is so important to know the scriptures. Jesus spoke the truth against the enemy (the culprit who puts us against each other). When we stand in position, we win battles, and He talks to us so that He gives us the words that will lead us into victory in that battle.

May 20

Grounded in Jesus

There are six things the Lord hates – no, seven things he detests: haughty eyes, a lying tongue, hands that kill the innocent, a heart that plots evil, feet that race to do wrong, a false witness who pours out lies, a person who sows discord in a family. (Proverbs 6:16-19)

Being grounded in Him is being dropped in truth; here in this verse is an example of what He does not approve of at all – running to do wrong with a heart to hurt someone else; let us think about this. We injured others directly, but we say we believe when we purposely do it, plan it, and follow through with it. We must be careful; this will never impress Him; it will never get you closer; instead, you will put yourself in a position of being more distant from Him. Is it worth it? Do we win the battle even if we think they deserve it? Do not sacrifice your invested walk with Jesus for anyone or anything. Trust Him because He fights our struggles, and He is the Judge. Our hearts have to stay pure as our capabilities allow us to (keeping it real). No one is perfect but please never be the initiator in hurting others or connected to them because you will be risking losing Jesus. Run to Him, do good, stay humble, and invite others to join you in this journey.

Intercede (prayer in favor of another)

Who then will condemn us? No one—for Christ Jesus died for us and was raised to life for us, and he is sitting in the place of honor at God's right hand, pleading for us. (Romans 8:34)

Healing is what we all desire. God is the only One who offers this healing. He gave us the gift of the Holy Spirit not just for us but also to intercede for those who He brings into our lives; may everyone know that they have a purpose. Whether it is who we wanted or not, God still uses that person or situation to show us something about ourselves. Maybe we were a blessing for them, but they did not see it or were distracted. Interceding carries someone else's load to God in prayer when life has knocked them down temporarily and helps them fight through or receive healing from their sins. Everyone needs someone to pray. For all who encouraged my family and me, I want to say thank you. If we align with God, our prayers are powerful and effective, so today, bless someone by interceding. Jesus intercedes daily for us, not because He has to but because to Him, we are worth it, and He loves us.

May 22

Progress

I don't mean to say that I have already achieved these things or that I have already reached perfection. But I press on to possess that perfection for which Christ Jesus first possessed me. No, dear brothers and sisters, I have not achieved it, but I focus on this one thing: Forgetting the past and looking forward to what lies ahead, I press on to reach the end of the race and receive the heavenly prize for which God, through Christ Jesus, is calling us. (Philippians 3:12-14)

Do not stop. Keep going. Only Jesus is perfect. Everyone must understand that. So, with that said, there is no comparison with others. Can others be at a different level in their journey? Absolutely. There are many personal reasons for that, but we all can go to the next level because of the Holy Spirit's gift. The Bible says to follow these steps to progress: "press on" (move those barriers or go through but do not stop), "focus" (one thing at a time), "forget the past" (cannot hold on to those times that crushed our hearts and minds for we are still standing), and "look ahead" (this requires trust and faith in Jesus). We do not need to know the plan; follow-through, and it will be okay. We all want the prize, which is Jesus who gives contentment, love, and hope. Make that a goal for each day to be a step toward progress with Jesus.

Called to Serve Someone

Now there was a believer in Damascus named Ananias. The Lord spoke to him in a vision, calling, "Ananias!" "Yes, Lord!" he replied. The Lord said, "Go over to Straight Street, to the house of Judas. When you get there, ask for a man from Tarsus named Saul. He is praying to me right now. I have shown him a vision of a man named Ananias coming in and laying hands on him so he can see again." (Acts 9:10-12)

Reading scripture is necessary to break down. We get the message, but even before that, for someone to be used mightily by God, someone else served Him by either relaying a statement by God, walking beside them, or helping when needed. Ananias (who was a believer) had to go to Saul (who was killing believers) and give a message. But God was before him. It does not mean we will not feel uncomfortable. Ananias was obedient and followed through. Had he not, we do not know where Saul would have been. But God chose Ananias to serve Saul (who became Paul). Being obedient will require trusting God, having faith, loving unconditionally, taking risks, being uncomfortable, not judging, supporting, not giving up on that person, and being a part of something bigger than us. Serving will help someone find God. Then, it keeps moving on to others. It is an honor to be a part of that process.

Transformed to Obediently Serve God

But the Lord said, "Go, for Saul is my chosen instrument to take my message to the Gentiles and to kings, as well as to the people of Israel. And I will show him how much he must suffer for my name's sake." (Acts 9:15-16)

Please read before and after this verse.

Saul went from wanting to kill believers to preaching to people. Yes, transformation is possible with God when we genuinely seek or are chosen. We may walk around and think, "Who me?" or "Why would He choose me?" Maybe we never explored who He was until He got us to our knees. That thinking does not come from God: if you are breathing, you have a purpose. Now we must understand that sometimes we are chosen, but because we are distracted or have not opened the door to Him, we may not be ready. Do you fear change? We must seek Him. He knows our capabilities. We must find it inside of us. Once we do, it is an automatic click. It is a rush of freedom and confidence within. Knowing what to do and following His will comes with a cost: yes, suffering, losing people, or challenges. But God is with us, so go for it.

Trusting God When Feeling Hopeless

Shadrach, Meshach, and Abednego replied, "O Nebuchadnezzar, we do not need to defend ourselves before you. If we are thrown into the blazing furnace, the God whom we serve is able to save us. He will rescue us from your power, Your Majesty. But even if he doesn't, we want to make it clear to you, Your Majesty, that we will never serve your gods or worship the gold statue you have set up." (Daniel 3:16-18)

Trusting in moments that challenge us and our faith is not easy but is expected from us as we take this journey forward. As you read in the story, three men refused to bow to other gods because they were faithful to our one true God. They were put in a furnace but never did the flames touch them due to God covering them. He is with us, but we need to hold on to His words. Do not let emotions get the best of you. Your yes to God is the yes that says, "Even if we go through hardships, obstacles, or situations that make us feel like we are burning inside, you are the God that will change these flames inside of us and replace them with your spiritual light that will protect our whole being." We must step forward–no looking back, no being confused even though we do not understand. We must know who we are and understand who tugs our hearts as we walk with confidence. We win our battles, but we get through them with our God.

May 26

Open minded to the things of God

Then he opened their minds to understand the Scriptures. (Luke 24:45)

That moment that Jesus appeared to the disciples. The Bible says that He opened their minds to understand the scriptures. When we seek in His word–that desperate desire for answers, but most importantly for comfort that He is with us–and read without distractions when it is not on a to-do list but the top of a priority list, our minds are opened. It should never be a burden to be in His word because of what He suffered on that cross. We might say it was a burden, but He felt we were worth the cost. If you read further in the passage, *"And now I will send the Holy Spirit, just as my Father promised. But stay here in the city until the Holy Spirit comes and fills you with power from heaven"* (Luke 24:49). Do we believe this? Are we walking with this mindset? Because that power in our hands will defeat anything, the enemy throws. What holds us back from using it? Have we not yet activated our hearts to it for a reason? Freedom happens when we start using this power. Who does not want that?

Nothing Before God

The LORD was very angry with Solomon, for his heart had turned away from the LORD, the God of Israel, who had appeared to him twice. He had warned Solomon specifically about worshiping other gods, but Solomon did not listen to the LORD's command. (1 Kings 11:9-10)

King Solomon had everything and chose to follow other gods–even though God warned him not to–instead of staying with the one and only God. At the moment, things may look so good that we risk what we have with God or others because we are searching for something that we will not find in the world. But we risk losing the blessing He brings at the moment. God warns us about what He wants us to stay away from because He knows our flesh is weak. He must be the chosen one among everything and everyone because He offers eternal life and is the giver of all we have (not just the material things but also the gifts of singing, teaching, ministering, playing sports, etc.). What am I saying? Do not risk losing Him for temporary satisfaction. In Him, if you truly seek, you find all that you need to be content.

Challenged

For you know that when your faith is tested, your endurance has a chance to grow. So let it grow, for when your endurance is fully developed, you will be perfect and complete, needing nothing. (James 1:3-4)

Some like challenges to an extent, but when the challenge gets tough, intimidating, or hits our emotions, we do not want it anymore. How much can we take before we break? Obstacle after obstacle, waiting for a change, or standing there and enduring it face-to-face because there is no other choice. The answer is Jesus. When we survive what we go through, something changes. Because we give it to Him, and, in return, our faith gets more assertive, and troubles get weaker. But that only happens if we trust Him, believe all His promises, and understand that He controls everything. Endurance takes patience, trust, tears (this is always welcome in His presence), hope, and faith that says, "I don't understand, but I know my God is before me and for me."

May 29

Strive

All athletes are disciplined in their training. They do it to win a prize that will fade away, but we do it for an eternal prize. (1 Corinthians 9:25)

To strive means to grow, develop well, succeed, advance, etc. We must have something that encourages us to want to strive toward Jesus. As you read, our walk is like being an athlete: we are running, but it is okay to walk if you must. The most important thing is not to stop striving for Jesus. Be disciplined in training. So, you must plan, train your mind with truth, pray to have the energy to teach, and strive to get to know His heart. He is the daily adrenaline we need to survive this world; no one will survive without this. Some may try, but without Him, we walk around spiritually empty, wasting away even though we may look good on the outside. Why not strive to be healthy in both areas so that you make it to the finish line to Jesus? Every uniquely made athlete will have different training, so persevere. The prize will be the same: Jesus.

Right Wisdom

For jealousy and selfishness are not God's kind of wisdom. Such things are earthly, unspiritual, and demonic. For wherever there is jealousy and selfish ambition, there you will find disorder and evil of every kind. (James 3:15-16)

Choose where your wisdom comes from;

we have to be careful as it states jealousy. Jealousy takes away peace; it consumes our thoughts, creates anger, bitterness, etc. Selfishness brings disorder and is spiritual (grudges, anxieties, panics, fears of not knowing your identity, confusion - hard time deciding, never satisfied - always trying to satisfy a need that God can only meet). These are individual insecurities that never have anything to do with the other person. God waits for us to ask for His wisdom; we cannot have the world mindset and serve others with the right hearts: the "I" must change to "us." The door in our hearts is open, but not to allow the enemy to come in. God waits daily for our decision, for the change of hearts and minds. His hand is ready to grab ours; patient He is. When we connect with God, contentment makes us complete.

No Payment Required

If I were doing this on my own initiative, I would deserve payment. But I have no choice, for God has given me this sacred trust. What then is my pay? It is the opportunity to preach the Good News without charging anyone. That's why I never demand my rights when I preach the Good News. (1 Corinthians 9:17-18)

Yes, the Good News is free. In this world, we pay for services but not for the Good News. It is a sacred trust from God that is deep and serious whenever you share about Him with others. This assignment of sharing the Good News can challenge us as we approach others; some of the walls of their hearts' are very thick that it will take longer to get through, but at least as we share, God starts breaking down inside. Yes, there is a cost of changing to His ways, letting go or giving up control of things, etc. Paul says it well; the reward for us is in the opportunity and honor I say in sharing Jesus without expectations of anything. Maybe that is what it is; when people get this free love from others, they cannot comprehend why someone would invest time in them as not everyone takes the time. I will tell you, why? Lost souls need to be found, restored, and unconditionally loved. God has entrusted us to accomplish this task.

F.E.A.R.

But because the midwives feared God, they refused to obey the king's orders. They allowed the boys to live, too. (Exodus 1:17)

God says we do not fear. Fear can paralyze your thoughts, physical body, and emotions. We want to focus on the opposite of what we know this word represents. F(avor) is what we want from God, so we should respect His ways. E(ternal) is the reward or prize at the end of our journey. A(ssurance) knows we will never be alone again once we make our choice for Jesus. R(estored) to a new being with a new Godly perspective happens when we say YES to Jesus. Yes, we need His guidance as we break from old ways that are not right; that does not show that He walks with us. It is all about Him. We are just seeds that need to be watered, molded, and tossed around so that we can grow to be strong, bold, and courageous people because that is how He made us be.

June 2

Edge of His Cloak

Just then a woman who had suffered for twelve years with constant bleeding came up behind him. She touched the fringe of his robe, for she thought, "If I can just touch his robe, I will be healed." Jesus turned around, and when he saw her he said, "Daughter, be encouraged! Your faith has made you well." And the woman was healed at that moment. (Matthew 9:20-22)

We may have heard about this woman in a desperate situation. Are you currently in a position that is overwhelming you? Let this be an encouragement. Sometimes we need to be in a specific case so that we can be in it with Him. We need to think, "If I can just touch His robe," I will get my answer. So, yes, we need to move, run, and leave behind those in the way to get to Him. Be desperate, determined, confident, bold, and okay with being uncomfortable. He knows. He is waiting to catch us, but we need to humble ourselves and show we cannot do it alone anymore. We need to admit that we have no more strength without Him, that our ways do not work. Jesus had no problem weeping– it is okay. It is at that moment that the healing starts and that the answers will come. At that moment, that faith increases. We must be strong, focused, determined, and have no fear of going through the crowd (some will be family or friends) to get to Him.

June 3

You Got What You Need

But you have received the Holy Spirit, and he lives within you, so you don't need anyone to teach you what is true. For the Spirit teaches you everything you need to know, and what he teaches is true-it is not a lie. So just as he has taught you, remain in fellowship with Christ. (1 John 2:27)

We look to others for direction in our journey, but we received the Holy Spirit. The verse says two things: 1) everything the Spirit teaches is true, so we do not have to worry about anyone playing with our hearts and minds. 2) the Spirit leads us to what we need to know. We do not need to know everything, but sometimes we feel we need to. Sometimes we need to get to the point of surrendering our control of things we really cannot handle and trust God. That is not easy, but it is possible if we want to change or we are tired of the same issues. If we stop filling this hole in our hearts meant for Jesus with other people, things, or our pride, we will find our answers. He will direct us to those answers.

Share Him

For we speak as messengers approved by God to be entrusted with the Good News. Our purpose is to please God, not people. He alone examines the motives of our hearts. (1 Thessalonians 2:4)

Sharing what Jesus has done for us makes us want to run up a mountain and shout. When we experience this divine moment, we cannot keep it in. We realize we do not always get answers, but we are mature enough to know our best interest and trust Him. Our job is to share who He is. It is right and worth it. We are to please Him, not others. The verse is correct: we are not to seek human praise at any point. We must have the courage and be firm when instructed to share who He is, especially when facing opposition (daily challenges/people who may not know who He is). Most importantly, to keep going is the only option. Remember, there is no going back because the blessings that He is waiting to give to us are ahead of us. So, let Him stretch you because it is in this moment when the best of who He created you to be will come out. Keep sharing Jesus; it is the best gift you can give to anyone you love or who needs to know HOPE.

June 5

Authentic

Jesus replied, "I tell you the truth, unless you are born again, you cannot see the Kingdom of God." (John 3:3)

Authentic means to be honest, trust-worthy, genuine, and your actual self. Does that make some of us uncomfortable? Sometimes we may be more accurate with certain people because a door of no judgment has opened, and it feels safe when you genuinely think they get you and allow you that space to stop pretending to be what you are not. This verse reminds us that we must leave our old self and enter our true self: yes, with Jesus. With this new self, we no longer have unrealistic expectations for people. You can stop faking it and be YOU–not perfect at all but created to be for so much more. Do not waste life fixating on what you want to be. What am I saying? Being authentic can make you feel guilty because part of you wants to fit in, so you do not lose others, but the other part created for God's will and purpose will overpower you. Worry only about what He thinks of you.

June 6

United in Spirit

He replied, "The Father alone has the authority to set those dates and times, and they are not for you to know. But you will receive power when the Holy Spirit comes upon you. And you will be my witnesses, telling people about me everywhere - in Jerusalem, throughout Judea, in Samaria, and to the ends of the earth." (Acts 1:7-8)

As soon as we get baptized (Spirit comes upon us), we go through this transformation deep inside us that only Jesus knows. God knows those emotions and stirs them within us, not to harm us but to heal us. It is overwhelming. When Jesus left earth, He told his disciples they will receive power in the form of the Holy Spirit (what can't we overcome?), and they will be witnesses, spreading and sharing everything they saw. We must share our testimonies, too. Again, there is no holding back. So many need this hope of Jesus, His touch of love, this comfort that only He provides, this understanding that only He can put in perspective for us. He was 100% human for a reason. We all know the Fruit of the Spirit; *"But the Holy Spirit produces this kind of fruit in our lives: love, joy, peace, patience, kindness, goodness, faithfulness, gentleness, and self-control. There is no law against these things!" (Galatians 5:22-23).* That is a place to start as we interact with people. Jesus knew and lived having to endure how people treated Him, but He never sinned. It is not easy to be disciples and witnesses, but this should be our daily goal. He endured much more for us.

No Stopping

No, despite all these things, overwhelming victory is ours through Christ, who loved us. (Romans 8:37)

In whatever struggle you are in, VICTORY is ours. The Holy Spirit is carrying us. It does not need to make sense. Continue moving with boldness and confidence toward our God, our only hope. Remember who you are, not weak but strong and capable. Be willing to listen to what God says to lay down at the altar. If it breaks you down and not inspire you, let it go because you hold back the blessings He has for you. Meanwhile, they are on hold until you decide. You belong to God forever. No one can change that unless you walk away. When we open our door (our hearts), it is because we need something to be changed, cleaned up, fixed, glued together, and restored to stronger than before.

Build

We should help others do what is right and build them up in the Lord. (Romans 15:2)

I love when God's word sticks out, such as this one verse. He is speaking to let us know to help others do right and build them up in the Lord. Yes, this is the goal for Christians, but sometimes it can be challenging. Still, help others as much as you can–not to gain anything but because God has helped us. We must do the same. Some may be resistant to accepting our help, and that is okay. Just let them know you are there if they need you. Stay on the sideline, like in a game, and if chosen, then step forward. Do right, always try, forgive as fast as you can; if you hurt someone, make it right, walk in the Spirit, and build them up in the Lord. Pour as much of Jesus as you can into them. Love unconditionally. Show them you are not perfect, so they do not have to be either in the presence of Jesus. Just be true to who you are in Jesus; do not allow yourself to accommodate others just because you think you must be accepted. Keep your spiritual heart shining so that it radiates and impacts others.

June 9

Our Scars Can Tell Our Story

From now on, don't let anyone trouble me with these things. For I bear on my body the scars that show I belong to Jesus. (Galatians 6:17)

Here it goes: every single scar you have on your body has a story behind it–from accidents or hardships that remind you God was there and helped you through. Yes, even scars of the heart. He showed the wounds of our sins when He resurrected to prove it happened, so He can say, "I died for you, and I am here." He had no problem in showing His disciples if they needed to see. So, our scars prove that He heals, restores, loves, and is for us and that He will never let us go. That is my prayer for all of you: hold on. He is working on your behalf, but it is His timing, not ours. Some scars are more profound than others, so it takes time, but they will never sting again when healed. Instead, it will remind you that you are an OVERCOMER. "Thank you, Jesus, for the cross, for laying it all down, for carrying our burdens so we can be free. May we share about our imperfections and give You glory always. Amen."

Do Not Forget

"But watch out! Be careful never to forget what you yourself have seen. Do not let these memories escape from your mind as long as you live! And be sure to pass them on to your children and grandchildren. (Deuteronomy 4:9)

It can be easy to forget what God has done for us in the past, but we should not. What do I mean? These moments are the ones you need to remember as you are struggling. They will get you through because you overcame them. "Do you remember being lost in life, and someone took the time to pour into you, so now you are saved?" It is so important not to forget because life can try to block it from our minds. Whatever situations you overcame in the past are reminders that you will overcome the ones right in front of you now. These moments of obstacles are part of your testimony that someday will be shared to help others. Ask God to keep you focused, inspired, and filled with the Spirit so that you overflow and never forget the day He said, "Hello, welcome to your new family. You will never walk alone again. You are loved and accepted." To become in the future, we must OVERCOME now.

June 11

Faithfully His

Through their faith, the people in days of old earned a good reputation. (Hebrews 11:2)

When you read Hebrews, you will see how many were faithful and obedient to do God's will. They were not perfect, but God chose them to accomplish what He needed. Risk can bring fear, but God was with them. They had to trust their faith because people did not understand why they followed God (the only one that needs to understand is YOU). When the pressure was on, I would think they pondered the risk of walking alone, knowing even family or friends don't understand. But God is worth it all–time, love, prayers, and tears. Everything you pour out to honor God, you will receive back in blessings within His timing. It will be worth it. It will empower you to keep going. It will teach you that He is always in control. Your faith will only get stronger as you seek to focus and partner with Him to do what He needs, which is restoring, loving, encouraging, serving, teaching, and saving souls who are desperately searching for His touch.

Thorn in My Flesh

If I wanted to boast, I would be no fool in doing so, because I would be telling the truth. But I won't do it, because I don't want anyone to give me credit beyond what they can see in my life or hear in my message, even though I have received such wonderful revelations from God. So to keep me from becoming proud, I was given a thorn in my flesh, a messenger from Satan to torment me and keep me from becoming proud. Three different times I begged the Lord to take it away. Each time he said, "My grace is all you need. My power works best in weakness." So now I am glad to boast about my weaknesses, so that the power of Christ can work through me. (2 Corinthians 12:6-9)

Sometimes God wants to know how we will handle things in moments of weakness to see if we trust Him. Will we stay obedient? Will we trust? Will we wait? Will we boast about situations that we got out of without mentioning or giving credit to God? What will be a thorn (physical and mental weakness, hardship, and the struggle to leave worldly things for Kingdom things)? Is He enough for our lives? Are we mad for having thorns, or are we okay with it, knowing that God will get the glory? God's power and grace must be our focus to deal with the deep-rooted pain of thorns. So, wait patiently with faith, hope, and even with your thorns because, in His timing, He will remove them. Even if He does not, that is another question: Will we still believe? In our weakest moments, He is strong. All we need to say is, "Jesus, help me."

His Battle Not Mine

When our enemies and the surrounding nations heard about it, they were frightened and humiliated. They realized this work had been done with the help of our God. (Nehemiah 6:16)

This one is hard at times because we go through frustration and impatience since we live in a world that says, "I want this issue in my life to be taken care of now." If He fights for us, we should not worry and stay focused on what He wants us to do: educating, loving, and being who He made us to be. If we take care of His business, He will take care of ours. All battles are challenging–big or small–the question is: Will you stand against it, give up, stay on the sidelines, or fight with Jesus? We have victory, but to be victorious requires strength, focus, courage, the armor of God without a single crack on it, and unconditional love to encourage us that things are worth fighting for if we have faith. Our marriages, children, families and friendships, identities, and testimonies are worth the fight. Remember- *"But you belong to God, my dear children. You have already won a victory over those people, because the Spirit who lives in you is greater than the spirit who lives in the world" (1 John 4:4).* So, lift your Bibles (swords), and start marching.

June 14

Jesus Set Boundaries

For we are each responsible for our own conduct.
(Galatians 6:5)

First, we need to be responsible for our conduct, not for Him but for us. You need to create a soul checklist of what you value and what is important to you: what God thinks, your family, your friends, co-workers, your church or your identity. You need to set boundaries to keep your mind on what keeps you focused. This way, you can be that role for everyone in your life. God uses us to pour into others. Jesus set boundaries. He spent time alone with God (as it should also remind us, we cannot do anything without Him), but I would think it was overwhelming at times. He spent so much time with people: healing the sick, listening to broken hearts, seeing so many hurt (physically, mentally, and emotionally) and mistreated. And He was calm, patient, and loved so deeply, and He loves us just the same. Leaders, I know you can relate to this. What are your boundaries? Do you know what you must do for you to be right in your mind, heart, and soul?

June 15

Not Our Words but His

I came to you in weakness-timid and trembling. And my message and my preaching were very plain. Rather than using clever and persuasive speeches, I relied only on the power of the Holy Spirit. I did this so you would trust not in human wisdom but in the power of God. (1 Corinthians 2:3-5)

The power of God is our daily drive. The core of our hearts will speak Jesus's words when in alignment with Him. As Paul shares, he is humble to the Holy Spirit as he tells them just as we should be. He shares with them that his words are plain and straightforward because they need to know who controls his speech. To share about Jesus, you do not need to speak with fancy words; share your testimony, the truth of what He has done for you. When you are in a position to share God's word, something in you feels like what he wrote in this verse, trembling and timid–not in the way of defeat but the form of triumph through God and dependence on Him. When he takes over your speech once you start, it is an honor to share. Wisdom is from God, so in all unanswered questions, seek Him for the answers. If you seek human knowledge, go to those who will guide you and lead you to His truth.

June 16

Believing in Him

Then Jesus told them, "I tell you the truth, if you have faith and don't doubt, you can do things like this and much more. You can even say to this mountain, 'May you be lifted up and thrown into the sea,' and it will happen. You can pray for anything, and if you have faith, you will receive it." (Matthew 21:21-22)

If you look at the meaning of "believe," it is to trust in something and accept it as authentic, genuine, and honest. I pray that your hearts are always excited for Jesus. God hears us, sees us, knows our hearts, and He will answer those prayers in His timing. Believe His promises, trust His words, and be still in waiting. Receive what God has for you: a word, a hug from someone, an answered prayer, or even a "let's wait for now" answer from Him. Expect something in your life to change so you are relieved from bondage. If you listen and have an open mind, you can share love unconditionally from those who accept, understand, know you, and care for you. Share your story if God moves you to, so that someone can be encouraged and find the hope they seek.

Approachable God

And we are confident that he hears us whenever we ask for anything that pleases him. (1 John 5:14)

The key point from this verse is to have confidence that He hears us. Reflect on the day He saved you because this is the day it all changed for us, the day we should never forget, the day we need to go back to when life gets tough, the day that reminds us to get back on track. Know that He loves you, and you were worth it. Share Him with others. Please be in His presence–not out of obligation, but soaking in all His peace, His overflowing love, His grace, and forgiveness that are so deep–to keep believing, trusting, enduring, hoping, and moving forward. May He move our hearts as we pray to Him honestly. Being in His presence should be the only thing that matters, where we lay it all. As we lean in, He will catch us, hold us, and pour more of Himself into us to the point of overflow so that we may run and share with the ones that are seeking.

June 18

Apply to Your Life

But don't just listen to God's word. You must do what it says. Otherwise, you are only fooling yourselves. (James 1:22)

God always points us in the right direction. To get straight to the point, do not just listen to what you hear, but follow it. Do not just take notes, highlight, or rewrite verses, but apply them to your life. It goes with everything we read to help us, guide us, encourage us, and build us up for this journey with Jesus. If God says, "Be Still," do it. Why? Because He knows the emotion of anger or anxiety will get the best of us, we may make a wrong decision or act without thinking. So, when He says wait, He is saying, "Trust me, believe in me, and I will guide you." Reading the Word and applying it helps direct our lives. The word of God not used will result in nothing being effective. Nothing will change. Doesn't that make you feel tired? Are you in the same place and not growing to the next level? Go to scripture and apply what you read.

June 19

Get Up

Then the angel of the LORD came again and touched him and said, "Get up and eat some more, or the journey ahead will be too much for you." So he got up and ate and drank, and the food gave him enough strength to travel forty days and forty nights to Mount Sinai, the mountain of God. (1 Kings 19:7-8)

We will sometimes get knocked down by the enemy. That one moment you were distracted, tired, busy, not prayed up, or fully armored can throw you off. What do you do with this? You got knocked down so hard; the enemy's fireball took you so far in the distance you landed on the floor in surprise. Before you get up, secure your armor, pray for God to send His direction and fireballs (Holy Spirit, verses, strength, protection) because the fight is on. If you are spiritually exhausted, sit and rest. Then get up but do not give up. You cannot give up, even if it hurts as you fight through. If equipped with Jesus, the next fireball will reverse that the enemy will get knocked down with flames. Again, GET UP, and DON'T GIVE UP. No matter what, stand your ground. VICTORY is ours.

June 20

No Division Allowed
in the House

If people are causing divisions among you, give a first and second warning. After that, have nothing more to do with them. For people like that have turned away from the truth, and their own sins condemn them. (Titus 3:10-11)

One God, one truth, one purpose. There will be times conflicts can try to hurt the body (the church), but this is the thing, stay in the mindset that – "We will keep it about Jesus and what he says." That keeps it in order, keeps it truthful, some will follow it, and some will not because they want to cause division but maybe because they are struggling within and do not realize it. What do we do? Pray, they see that turning away from the truth and the body (the church) that needs them will not benefit them. Everyone is essential; some run faster to the altar; it is okay to walk there as long as you get there and give Him the glory. The word says, let them go after warnings; that is the truth as we all have had moments of figuring things out. Consequently, we have free will, but it does not always end up in goodwill decisions. Let us keep it about "Jesus" always, so we stay on track.

Under His Care

The LORD will guide you continually, giving you water when you are dry and restoring your strength. You will be like a well-watered garden, like an ever-flowing spring. (Isaiah 58:11)

So true story: I was pondering on a decision I had to make and praying to God for direction. If you are in His presence daily, you should know there will be times His response is immediate. He knows you are struggling with a hard decision, so He will help you out so that you can continue moving forward. That is what happened. I received a text from a good friend that very night. We usually text in the morning, so it was a reminder to put me back on track and eased the pressure I was feeling. What is the point? God always helps those who seek Him. It is okay to have a weak moment. He wants us to be who we are at all times. There is no faking it; be honest. He makes it clear that He will send you help, but then you must keep going. We have work to do—no quitting or giving up because He is with you always, even when you ponder.

June 22

Lord, Save Me

But when he saw the strong wind and the waves, he has terrified and began to sink. "Save me, Lord!" he shouted. Jesus immediately reached out and grabbed him. "You have so little faith," Jesus said, "Why did you doubt me?" (Matthew 14:30-31)

There are moments when we take our eyes off Jesus because we think we can handle the storms of life. Peter took his eyes off Jesus, so he began to sink. Have you ever been in that position? It is okay. Get up and refocus. Figure out where you lost sight of Him, so you are aware of it, and try to avoid being in that position again. We all lose sight. Not one of us is exempt from this. The question is: How do you handle this? Pray, read, or be in silence, without music or anything, away from all the voices that pull you. Sometimes we need to step back from that situation we are in to see the cause of our struggles. It is not easy because you now must take action or accountability for something you could have avoided. But you know it, call on Jesus to redirect your step, to calm your storm. He will grab your hand when you call but be willing to take His direction for which way to go without doubting. Just have FAITH.

June 23

Secure His Words in Your Heart

My child, never forget the things I have taught you. Store my commands in your heart. If you do this, you will live many years, and your life will be satisfying. (Proverbs 3:1-2)

What does this verse mean? The heart pumps blood all over our body so that it functions. God's word is like that. When we read His word, it fills our spirit and brings this same excitement of wanting to move our body parts. An example is using our mouths to talk about Him, pray to Him, or sing for Him. We use our hands to hold someone in need, to serve, or to clap in praise. We use our ears to hear someone in need or to hear His voice. Our legs run to the altar for more. When filled with His words, our hearts keep us wanting more, keep us feeling alive even in the worst moments, and keep our minds focused on what is good. How can we feel defeated? God always wins—no questions on that. There is no room for any emotions other than unconditional love when we focus on His promises. Focus on your "true love," which keeps your heart overflowing, who mended it back together, who tells you when to be guarded or when it is safe to be open.

June 24

Gap of Righteousness

"I looked for someone who might rebuild the wall of righteousness that guards the land. I searched for someone to stand in the gap in the wall so I wouldn't have to destroy the land, but I found no one. So now I will pour out my fury on them, consuming them with the fire of my anger. I will heap on their heads the full penalty for all their sins. I, the Sovereign LORD, have spoken!" (Ezekiel 22:30-31)

At a time when leaders who were supposed to lead Israel were not doing what God expected them to do. So, God was searching for someone to step up to fight for the injustices that have occurred, someone willing to stand in the gap where others cannot or will not. Some did not know due to feelings of fear, lack of confidence, or weakness by overpowering people, and some did not honor God's command. Because God found no one to stand, consequences will occur. We must stand when we can for those who need help and stand for God in areas we know He would not want us to walk away and leave unsettled. How would you know? The Holy Spirit will stir you to move where you thought you never would. It overpowers you to step up, and so you do it. Jesus stood in the gap for us to make it right with God. He is our example of someone who cared.

June 25

Walking with Dignity

She is clothed with strength and dignity, and she laughs without fear of the future. (Proverbs 31:25)

Dignity is essential to who you are. It is a sense of pride in oneself. Be proud of what you were blessed with and bless others with that gift. Having dignity is not being selfish. Dignity is self-respect, self-worth, and confidence in your spirit. God created us with specific characteristics: some are the strengths that help us survive, and some are the weaknesses we need to work on, but He still uses both for His purposes and will help us tweak those weaknesses into strengths. Yes, we are all flawed (imperfect), in need of Jesus (the only perfect being) to fix us. The verse states, she is "clothed with strength and dignity." Yes, covered with God's presence. So, every time you see "she," replace it with your name. Being surrounded by God's presence makes us feel solid and secure and helps us walk with this feeling of confidence. Sometimes it might scare you because that fear you carried before is gone—which feels weird because it was a norm in your life—but no more. Now you have strength and dignity.

Searching for Level of Faith

Abraham never wavered in believing God's promise. In fact, his faith grew stronger, and in this he brought glory to God. He was fully convinced that God is able to do whatever he promises. And because of Abraham's faith, God counted him as righteous. (Romans 4:20-22)

Imagine birds flying; one is the leader, and the others follow. Some are trying to catch up with all their might as the wind comes full force. Apply this to how our journey is: the wind is the struggles or challenges of life. Abraham, the father of many nations, became a father when he was old. But all that time, he kept his faith. It did not weaken in this situation that seemed hopeless. Do you know what I am saying? He kept hoping and believing God's promises were true. Waiting is a part of this journey. It says no wavering. His faith just grew more assertive in this waiting. There is always a leader and followers, all scattered but still will be behind the leader. We are all at different levels in our faith but yet following our one, true God? You see, striving, pushing harder, and maintaining focus will get you closer to the leader (God). Are you seeking, doing all that you can to move faster? Do you want that next level with more cost?

Do not let anyone or anything stop you from getting to the next level. He gets all the glory in each exact moment in your story.

June 27

Released to Live

You have died with Christ, and he has set you free from the spiritual powers of this world. So why do you keep on following the rules of the world, such as, "Don't handle! Don't taste! Don't touch!"?
(Colossians 2:20-21)

What does "to die with Christ" mean to you? To die means to lose one's life and give up our plan. Have you let go of your life to accommodate God? Where are you at with Him? What is this life bringing you? Being who we were can slowly let our struggles of doubt consume us. We need to give it to God to direct everything and let Him define our new identity. Jesus laid down His life for us. Would you lay down your life for someone? Would you put your selfish ways on hold? Would you help someone in the capacity that God wants you to be and depart this life (not physically, but mentally and emotionally)? That is the way we survive. We cannot go into the world thinking and saying, "I'm a Christian," but not living it out. It does not go anywhere. Stop being fooled. Do you lean on Him, who encourages you, or are you always taking the lead? Let God take over your dying self.

Just Ask Jesus

"What do you want me to do for you?" Jesus asked. "My Rabbi, "the blind said, "I want to see!" And Jesus said to him, "Go, for your faith has healed you." Instantly the man could see, and he followed Jesus down the road. (Mark 10:51-52)

It is not complicated; we make it hard; we live this life constantly struggling for Him to help us, but we hold the answer within the whole time, yes, the Holy Spirit. It is within us for a reason, to guide us, comfort us, clarify, alert when we are doing something we should not be doing, and encourage, so we do not get stuck in this discouraging world. Jesus asked the blind man what He needed as we know it was to see. When we have faith (reliance, loyalty, or complete trust in God) in a God, we do not see but knows our hearts so well, especially our faith level – nothing is impossible. The blind man just heard Jesus was nearby and shouted loud enough to be heard by Him. Is anyone calling Jesus to help? "Jesus, lead us to the next level." Yes, the blind man received the healing because he knew Jesus was the answer. Does anyone believe it? Is anyone tired of searching? If so, call out to Jesus, and you will find Him.

June 29

Soulfully Times

This is what the LORD says: "Stop at the crossroads and look around. Ask for the old, godly way, and walk in it. Travel its path, and you will find rest for your souls. But you reply, 'No, that's not the road we want!' (Jeremiah 6:16)

Use your time soulfully. What do I mean?

As you come to a crossroad of what to do with your time in a given moment, choose to fill your cup (your soul) with Jesus's presence: a song, your Bible, prayer time, standing in the gap for a friend who needs it, or just sitting in solitude and hearing Him say, "I am here with you; you are never alone." All these moments are necessities for your soul to be maintained and should not be moments of "Whenever I have time, I will get to it." Can I be honest? This place of peace, security, hope, love, growth, seeking, and identity in Jesus is where we need to be. Let us keep each other in prayer and may God hear each one and answer in His timing.

June 30

Acknowledging our Wrong

If I had not confessed the sin in my heart, the Lord would not have listened. But God did listen! He paid attention to my prayer. (Psalm 66:18-19)

It is in the Word, so we must discuss it. God needs us to admit or acknowledge our wrongs so He can hear us, help, and guide us, elevate us, bless us, etc., but most of the times, the enemy will make us feel God will not forgive us, well that is not true, our Father is righteous and forgiving, but He is also Holy. He cannot be involved in anything or anyone attached to unholiness; that is why we must come and confess, so it opens that bridge for Him to enter. We hinder our elevation further in the Kingdom, our blessings, and risk losing a prayer when we seek sin. But this opens up another conversation amongst us, do we affect others' prayers from being heard if it comes from someone that has not confessed to God? "Forgive us, God. We are not perfect, and we aim to be the followers with pure hearts when we pray to You so that all of our prayers are heard and answered according to Your will. Amen."

July 1

Direction of Words

It is the same with my word. I send it out, and it always produces fruit. It will accomplish all I want it to, and it will prosper everywhere I send it. (Isaiah 55:11)

I always think of God's word as a fastpitch ball. Yes, like in baseball. When we throw the ball (God's word), it is quick and tossed with a force so that you feel the impact as it hits the glove (our hearts). We need to make sure we catch God's word as He throws them our way. It will produce fruit and accomplish what He wants it to complete. We must do what is expected of us to help others grow in their journey who do not know who God is. But for words to be sent out and produced, we must be alert and willing to listen—blocking out all those noises surrounding us that distract us from hearing or accomplishing anything. God will help us to listen to His words, and may they be loud and clear so we can prosper.

July 2

Set Your Spirit

So letting your sinful nature control your mind leads to death. But letting the Spirit control your mind leads to life and peace. (Romans 8:6)

Keep your eyes on Jesus. Even though the flesh pulls, we must try not to give in if what we seek is a peaceful life. Both cannot rule, direct, and move your life; you must make a choice. Do you want to go into continuous destruction of yourself as you walk into the fire (anything that goes against what God's standards are)? Or do you want to be the one who turns off the fire of destruction with the winds of God's word so that you can rise above it? It is not easy to do, but it is not impossible either when God leads us, directs us, and creates us with a characteristic of overcoming that we must figure out how to activate (yes, it takes work of obedience, trust, faith, hope, and love). You decide your outcome. Do not let anyone make your decision. You are more than what you think.

July 3

Testing Will Squeeze You

God blesses those who patiently endure testing and temptation. Afterward they will receive the crown of life that God has promised to those who love him. (James 1:12)

How many times are you in a position that life feels like you are on a roller coaster of trials, of testing who you are and who you desire to represent truly? When on that ride, the twists and turns throw you off because even though you knew something was coming, you did not know how or when? In our journeys, testing is part of the plan. The question is: how are you going to handle it? Are you going to stop, drop, and not move? Or are you going to run to His word and read what will empower you not to give in but get up? You see, in the end, there is a prize (crown of life). We know we have eternal life, but it is more than that. With every trial that comes, we get blessed because we know it is a test we will not fail if our faith level is high. You must seek Him more than anything; there is never too much of God. Be patient during the test, learn from it, and endure it. Tears are allowed but keep going.

Who is Teaching You Truth?

Teach me your ways, O LORD, that I may live according to your truth! Grant me purity of heart, so that I may honor you. (Psalm 86:11)

I hope you have this answer: Yes, Jesus. Pray, He directs your steps to seek Him, as He is the only way. There is no other. We can try to replace His spot in our hearts, but they (a person, jobs, money, fill in the blank: _____) will never be an exact match, love, or truth that He represents. Nothing else will click in your heart. We ask to live in God's reality, but this is a struggle because our hearts and behaviors must be pure to live this. The battle is between worldly temporary now or future eternal blessings. Does He abide in us, or does He not? Do we dream of changing, or do we truly seek it? May we follow what God will teach us to genuinely follow His truth and not have divided hearts that never get healed.

July 5

Rising Above It All

Those who love your instructions have great peace and do not stumble. (Psalm 119:165)

God will always walk before us and give us bold steps. You must know God to believe this because if you do not, you will crumble. Rising above is like going against solid winds (name your battles) that come your way. As it comes, you move toward it; you push back—even as your steps lose balance— you keep trying. There is no backing down. Here it goes: daily, weekly, or monthly, something may come up, or we sin, and we end up at a crossroad. Do we run back because we do not want to face it, or do we go forward and through because God is saying we must keep going as part of our journey? It takes knowing yourself, trusting God, and pushing through with all you got emotionally, mentally, and physically. Be prepared: not everyone gets it, but they will understand if they seek God as you do. Most importantly, His peace is what carries you.

Do You Have a Seed You Carry?

But the wisdom from above is first of all pure. It is also peace loving, gentle at all times, and willing to yield to others. It is full of mercy and the fruit of good deeds. It shows no favoritism and is always sincere. And those who are peacemakers will plant seeds of peace and reap a harvest of righteousness. (James 3:17-18)

We have heard if we pour little into something, we will receive little. This wisdom we receive has many benefits that will help us if we allow it to direct our hearts. Knowledge is not selfish; it chooses its battles, as some are not worth fighting if what we can lose is greater. It is pure; nothing is mixed, and no grey areas. It aims to be a peacemaker so that its outcome brings good. Wisdom shows us how to be transparent because being who we are is how God created us. Why do some strive to be people that He does not recognize because we are not walking in His ways? Forgiven is what this wisdom tells us we are if we truly repent. What does it take to turn back? More tears? More loss or confusion? It is never too late to be the person who seeks God's wisdom. He is still there. Find your mustard seed, allow it to grow, then pass it on to others.

July 7

Not Even One

And this is the will of God, that I should not lose even one of all those he has given me, but that I should raise them up at the last day. (John 6:39)

Jesus led the ones who were going to follow. The invitation to Jesus is for everyone. But not everyone takes it. Remember, there is a cost of letting go and changing. Or the timing is not now. God's will is our will, so we must have the same goal of not losing one God has put on our path. Just be, listen, or direct, and do not stop praying for them. You will see God move and change situations and mindsets. To know that Jesus will not let go of us should be comforting, especially when He is all we have in certain moments. Not losing even one means not giving up on "those" people. So yes, it can be challenging, but you do not walk alone. So, take the invitation for the assignment. Others are waiting for you for those specific moments and reasons.

Must We See to Really Believe?

Then Jesus told him, "You believe because you have seen me. Blessed are those who believe without seeing me." (John 20:29)

How many are out there and have thought or still think like Thomas, who needed to touch Jesus's wounds to believe that it was Him? He loved Jesus, but he needed to see and experience it to believe it. We cannot touch Him, but we hold on to the promises He made and are in the Bible to keep us encouraged. Sometimes, our faith gets tested, yes, but when everything goes wrong, our attitude turns to faithless thinking if we are not seeking God. Can I be honest? Being a follower is challenging, especially during those hits that tug the heart so much that all we can do is shed tears and endure because we know "Blessed are those who believe without seeing" is a promise. Do we need more than that? He said it, and so it is. Believing in who He is and what He can do for us starts the healing, restoration, and breakthrough process in any situation.

Earthly Loneliness but Spiritually Prayed Up?

Then Jesus said to the crowd, "Am I some dangerous revolutionary, that you come with swords and clubs to arrest me? Why didn't you arrest me in the Temple? I was there teaching every day. But this is all happening to fulfill the words of the prophets as recorded in the Scriptures." At that point, all the disciples deserted him and fled. (Matthew 26:55-56)

We all know the story of Jesus's betrayal from not only the one that was responsible for the act but also from all those who left Him. He was human, so please understand that what we feel, He feels. He felt that moment when no one was praying for Him because of being distracted by their physical need. They were not in tune with the spiritual part of themselves to cover Jesus in prayer. When we can pray for others: do it because it is crucial. Take the time. That one prayer can shift the heart from hopelessness to faith, discomfort to encouragement, weakness (earthly perspective) to becoming spiritually strong. Our flesh is weak. That is why we constantly must have our minds soaking into the Word to keep us strong. Even when we feel alone, this is a reality; we will not always have someone there—all we need is Jesus. Be prepared to uplift others spiritually.

July 10

Committed Body

Don't you realize that all of you together are the temple of God and that the Spirit of God lives in you? (1 Corinthians 3:16)

Hmm, meditate on this: we are His temple, and we carry the Holy Spirit within us. It is an important responsibility we have. Our bodies belong to Him. What do we do with that which is not of Him? If we follow it, we will be disrespecting Him, not only ourselves; that is the truth. We were created and chosen to lead and help others to come to Him. Now, if we do not, then we will see the difference in someone who does. The Spirit stretches us to places or people because there is a mission, but as it happens, it challenges us in our walk. This journey is not suppose to be easy; it intends to change ways, impact lives, heal, restore, and transform. If someone is struggling, I pray you do not give up but stand up. Let go of what trips you and lean into Jesus.

Battle Ready

But you will not even need to fight. Take your positions; then stand still and watch the LORD's victory. He is with you, O people of Judah and Jerusalem. Do not be afraid or discouraged. Go out against them tomorrow, for the LORD is with you!"
(2 Chronicles 20:17)

We must engrave this in our minds, hearts, or even on sticky notes—whatever it takes to get in. As you read, a battle was going to happen. But God says, "I will be with you." That is it. Do you have a war going on right now? The verse says, "take your position, then stand still and watch the LORD's victory." Let us think about this. So, if we get knocked down, you mean to get back up, God? Yes. What if pushed out of our position, you mean reposition ourselves? Yes. I know you get it, as the message is clear: no fear allowed. Just walk knowing and trusting-no backing down, especially with life's challenges (battles). We will encounter new goals that seem impossible for us, but not for our God. No matter how many times we need to stand up against something, do it. Never let the enemy win a battle that you know God won. He may distract us if we are not aware of his schemes, but he will not succeed unless you stay down.

July 12

Do not Hold Back

For I long to visit you so I can bring you some spiritual gift that will help you grow strong in the Lord. When we get together, I want to encourage you in your faith, but I also want to be encouraged by yours. (Romans 1:11-12)

Paul wrote a letter to a church in Rome. He always prayed for them, heard of them, and wanted to see them so that he could pour into them. We each have a unique gift that no one else can master; they will help others, so use it. You will see Paul wants to pour out and wants them to pour in; this is so important. We are to build each other up, pray for each other, and when we gather with other believers, we learn new things about ourselves and diverse perspectives that we never thought of before. When we get to that place of wanting to share about Jesus, we get stronger in our faith, we know that to get to help others grow in their faith is an honor. We learn from each other, and if you do not understand something, ask God for wisdom, patience, and guidance along the way. Pour out your gifts and receive others' contributions of what God has gifted them to share with others. Then watch your faith grow to move hearts.

Do We Have a Strategy (Plan of Action to Achieve an Aim)?

So don't go to war without wise guidance; victory depends on having many advisers. (Proverbs 24:6)

We must always have a plan in whatever we do. When we shop, we plan to make a list. When we carpool our children, we get up early and do what we need to do to get everyone to their destinations. If we have an event, we plan to ensure we have everything that we need to orchestrate all details. So, do we have a plan to defend ourselves from the enemy? As giants (fear, distractions, hopelessness, built-up anger, or disappointments) present themselves, how can anyone get through these without Jesus? The verse says we do not go to war without wise guidance (Who can this be?). Jesus must guide us. We cannot win a war without a plan of action.

Be Unstoppable

"I know that you can do anything, and no one can stop you. (Job 42:2)

Job had confidence and assurance in God that he can do all things and that He is unstoppable. What does this mean? That unbeatable feeling is in me? If God is so, then it means I am too? Yes, and yes. We must believe that the One we belong to will step in for the ones we love or us. Some give up because they get to a certain point in a situation where it seems that nothing is changing. But why? Have you honestly been crying out to Him, or is it just a cliché prayer that sounds good? The same old way of thinking and acting must go. There is no negotiation here, or we stay stuck. Do not stop praying, even when you feel like life is just twirling you around in confusion or the enemy is grabbing your loved ones. The enemy may think he has what will break you until he sees you are more powerful than ever. Unstoppable prayers will be answered but do you have an unconquerable spirit even with discouraging people around? Be confident and assured that you could do anything in Christ.

July 15

Imitator

So whether you eat or drink, or whatever you do, do it all for the glory of God. (1 Corinthians 10:31)

Many may think this is not a problem, but sometimes there is division in churches. Here it goes, everything we do – no matter what it is, if we want this walk, then we must glorify God, no negotiating on this. We are not to offend the churches of God. Our goal is to get closer to Him and help others find their way; we won't understand this part until we meet that one person. That is reaching out their hand for us to grab, that does not have a light inside – constantly in darkness, so no love or identity is inside their heart – this is sad, and we should feel it that deep. Be imitators of Christ but know we will never be perfect like Him, but be the best servant you can for others. God sends them to us to find their way to be saved, and He knows we will help. It is never about us, but others turn it around and criticize it. We cannot change their insecurities – stay focus. God knows the ones that pour out selflessly for others.

Everyone Matters

When he arrived and saw this evidence of God's blessing, he was filled with joy, and he encouraged the believers to stay true to the Lord. Barnabas was a good man, full of the Holy Spirit and strong in faith. And many people were brought to the Lord. (Acts 11:23-24)

If you read before this verse, because believers shared who God was, many people found their salvation. But what if they were selfish and did not share? Many would have been missing out, still wandering, still searching for this God who people pray to, seek, and love, who unconditionally loves us back. This God forgives and heals (our hearts, emotional ups and downs, our thinking) gives us the strength to keep moving forward. When we remember what God did for us, we should be running, not walking, to help others. We will receive what the verse says: God's blessings, joy, encouragement, the Holy Spirit. We must stay strong in our faith, especially during hardships. Our faithfulness will help the ones who are faithless. It is an honor that He places us specifically to be around others when He knows you are the only one who can lead them to Him. Say yes and do it.

No Words

And the Holy Spirit helps us in our weakness. For example, we don't know what God wants us to pray for. But the Holy Spirit prays for us with groanings that cannot be expressed in words. And the Father who knows all hearts knows what the Spirit is saying, for the Spirit pleads for us believers in harmony with God's own will. (Romans 8:26-27)

Sometimes, during our lives, especially the loss of someone close to us or when things keep falling out of alignment, some may think to themselves, what did I do to deserve this? How about this, instead: it is a part of life. We do not and will not understand, but we endure without saying a word because no words can express what we want to say to God. This verse reminds us that the Spirit groans (a deep sound conveying pain or despair). We all have experienced a loss of a loved one, a broken relationship, and moments of confusion—maybe about which voice to listen to, or even try to do the right thing as we break away from the wrong, something we know is injuring our soul. He is our wonderful Counselor in the moments when we cannot say a word or even when we have temporarily given up. "Thank you, Holy Spirit, for communicating the words we can't get out." God is never surprised when we are at that place, and He always listens.

Trembling Inside

He shakes the earth from its place, and its foundations tremble. (Job 9:6)

Has anyone ever felt that out-of-control trembling (shaking involuntarily because of anxiety, excitement, or frailty)? When it happens, you find yourself unable to control the movement or your body's intensity, whether moving slowly or quickly. Some can relate to that feeling you had inside when God captured your heart. Emotions were up in the air once you invited Him in as He shook your insides to renew your spirit and soul. God will never share space with anyone or anything because He is God. Sometimes we need those trembling moments to understand what God is doing. As the verse says, He shakes the earth out of its place, just like He does to us. Maybe to get our attention or remind us that He is in charge. Or perhaps it is needed to put us on the path He is directing us to. Trust Him because that power He gives us is what we walk with, and even when we tremble, we got this; let everything that is not of Him go away.

Winning Team

And we are instructed to turn from godless living and sinful pleasures. We should live in this evil world with wisdom, righteousness, and devotion to God, while we look forward with hope to that wonderful day when the glory of our great God and Savior, Jesus Christ, will be revealed. (Titus 2:12-13)

There are two teams: one is God's, and the other is the enemy. Why do we meddle in the enemy's team when we know it will never win? He has a game plan to cheat by tripping us up, but we expect it to make us happy. Is it reasonable to be wrong? You must be very alert so that you are one step ahead to block any moves. Live right (in your thoughts, actions, behaviors, and perspectives). We cannot mold people to think like us, but just maybe, if they see how devoted we are to God, it can help the world one heart at a time. We should not devote ourselves to people or things more than to God. So, take in His words, be good as much as you can (yes, sometimes you mess up, but God knows your heart, so no worries), and serve Him genuinely and authentically.

July 20

World

Watch out that you do not lose what we have worked so hard to achieve. Be diligent so that you receive your full reward. (2 John 8)

Our daily battle. Sometimes you will be at a crossroads of decisions, deciding whether to go to the left (worldly desires, your flesh, false identity) or the right (God's expectations, truth, His plans, your identity). There are always two options: either we walk and speak or think we know Jesus but deny Him by our words and actions. Think about your faith. Is it weak, lukewarm, or strong? Are you accommodating others to be loved or accepted? Are you breaking slowly or holding on to God? The verse says to be careful not to lose what you have worked hard to achieve. Here it goes; we work hard to keep this faith, be truthful, have hope, and not negotiate our time with God because He is worth it and holds our reward. For anyone to follow our lead, they must see in us that faith, obedience, and consistency in His presence. No religion, no God. Choose to go to the right at that crossroad. There you will find Jesus.

Hands That Hold Up

Yet I still belong to you; you hold my right hand. You guide me with your counsel, leading me to a glorious destiny. Whom have I in heaven but you? I desire you more than anything on earth. (Psalm 73:23-25)

There is something about holding hands that empowers us. We do not need words for it. It comforts us when we need support or helps us keep standing up in rough moments. It unifies us to pray for others and to be prayed for, which locks in our prayer chain. The verse says, "Yet I still belong to you; you hold my right hand." Yes, God holds us, even when our grip is weak due to our rebellious moments. His grip means, "I got you, I know you, and I know what you want, but I'm going to give you what you can handle for now." His grip says, "I know you are struggling with yourself, others, and stretching moments I have allowed in your life, but what I want for you to know is that I have your hand. So, if you slip, it's okay; I got you." God will lead all areas of our lives, but will you let Him guide you? Put Him above all, and you will see that God will never let you go if you hold on.

July 22

Rewarding for Enduring

"God blesses you when people mock you and persecute you and lie about you and say all sorts of evil things against you because you are my followers. Be happy about it! Be very glad! For a great reward awaits you in heaven. And remember, the ancient prophets were persecuted in the same way. (Matthew 5:11-12)

As soon as we said yes to Jesus, the enemy said, "no way." He will not let us go that easy. How do you know? By the way, people start treating you differently. The new person you became can make others uncomfortable, causing them to distance themselves from you. Maybe it is not you. Perhaps it is the feeling of their guilt over how they are living. Then here we come, loving, praying, and praising God. People can stumble us by being mean and making fun of our beliefs or our new community. What do we do with that? People may knock us or disrespect us, giving us more power to continue praising God more. When we stand for God, no matter what, He will bless us with an excellent reward. We are not to be ashamed of who He is. Being His follower is worth everything we endure because He was treated like that but took more.

July 23

Declared

The LORD says, "Then I will heal you of your faithlessness; my love will know no bounds, for my anger will be gone forever. (Hosea 14:4)

People stay away from God or stop growing in their faith because of faithlessness, limited thinking, or even fear of God's anger. What is God saying that He will not be angry? Does it mean He will not hold grudges? He says that He forgave our sins no matter what we have done (of course, we all know we need to repent for our actions against Him). To overturn faithlessness, we can start by having an open mind and heart. Open your eyes and see where in your world He is present. Pray for that, and He will show you, but most importantly, may He heal whatever caused you to stumble. The love He provides is to infinity and beyond. We can expect that from some people, but it will never compare, as earthly love may consist of boundaries (limits).

Spiritually Survived

The human spirit can endure a sick body, but who can bear a crushed spirit? (Proverbs 18:14)

Sometimes in our seasons, our spirits get crushed. At that point, you have to make a decision; either we keep persevering or drown in what has crushed us. Is it easy? No, and that is ok; we must show our humanity as Jesus did. We endure the words or actions of others and carry what to do, no way around it, but God prepares us for these moments by understanding that He took more than what we have. We all have different levels of how to endure, but we should be trying to get power from one source. When you feel your spirit is at that point, find comfort that the Trinity is there. Still, the Trinity allows you to process everything as they surround and protect you from getting more damaged inside. It reminds you that this is just another moment we must go through; it is part of your story; you will make it because of who you are-His child that knows He will give you that strength needed.

Torn Knees Will Be Answered

But when Daniel learned that the law had been signed, he went home and knelt down as usual in his upstairs room, with its windows open toward Jerusalem. He prayed three times a day, just as he had always done, giving thanks to his God. (Daniel 6:10)

I hope you read before this verse to see Daniel was a Godly man who was consistent in prayer, trustworthy, and not involved in things that would dishonor God. Why is it wrong to do the right things for God? Keep going; God sees you. He is there when we slip; He knows people will try to trip you for loving Him. It is what you have in your hearts. You must be showing peace that people cannot understand, or they see your consistency in your journey following a God that you do not see, like Daniel (He prayed on his knees three times daily to thank God). Worshiping God was the only way they could charge Him with breaking the law, so what does he do now, pray the same way but with different words, of course, "help me," as he knows what will happen in desperate times. God will always answer if we are right with Him. But, if on our knees is all we got, then He says, "I'm coming."

Hearing or Doing?

For merely listening to the law doesn't make us right with God. It is obeying the law that makes us right in his sight. (Romans 2:13)

Is there a difference between hearing and doing? Absolutely. Hearing God's word is good; it is truth, comforting, encouraging, powerful, calm during the storm inside us, and not one thing can compare to it. So, if all that comes with just hearing the word of God, how much more powerful would it be to do what His word says? You see, there is a difference. Please do not fool yourselves. We are running toward the blessing. Being a doer of the Word will be a challenge because detachment from the world must happen. Doing is not only listening but also seeking, praying, honoring His commands, and taking His covenant seriously. What does it take for us to decide? We do not choose the rules, but He designed us to follow them if we genuinely want to say we are followers of Jesus. Do what you need to do to get one step closer to Jesus today.

Rewritten Script

Come and listen, all you who fear God, and I will tell you what he did for me. (Psalm 66:16)

Yes, our testimonies are our rewritten stories—once lost and now found, once broken, and now healed—if only we had allowed Him to dig deep into those areas that take us back to our old selves. Sit back for a second and think about where you are right now. What can you change? Do you have control to change others? Okay, here it goes; only God can change the script of your life. Stop trying so hard. He can add someone or remove someone. He can place you as a leader in a role or be an extra in the story (which is okay sometimes). Our rewritten stories are part of fixing where things went wrong to give us another chance. But this time, our story is written by God. He did have the original script, but we will always fall short if our faith is weak or compromises to fit in with the world. Yes, your testimony is your story. Some have lost their way and are stuck, needing a rewrite. Thank you, Jesus, for being the writer.

July 28

Independent with Him

For the LORD is our judge, our lawgiver, and our king.
He will care for us and save us. (Isaiah 33:22)

Being free and united, self-dependent and unwavering: that is what the United States is all about. Okay, so you know where I am going with this. Apply it to our walk with Jesus. Although we have free will, we need to always choose Him. But the beauty of this is, as you see in the verse. He is the One who creates our laws (this is the Bible), decides what is right or wrong (His instructions and explanation of the cost for our actions). And is the only One we follow (God does not share His position with anyone; He is the only King, Judge, Peacemaker, and Comforter). We are free but cannot be independent without Him because salvation only comes from Him.

Strong Tower

The name of the LORD is a strong fortress; the godly run to him and are safe. (Proverbs 18:10)

"God, you are a solid tower for us." A tower is many things:

** It can hold you up.
** It can reach and rise high.
** It can be a place of safety inside
** It is strong.

Well, you already know what I will say. Yes, God is the strong Tower that holds us up, which is higher than anyone. When we are in tune with His word, walking obediently and humbly with Him by our side, we will always RISE above anything that comes our way. He is our shelter when we think we cannot go any longer. Step back in His presence for rest or recovery from what knocked you down until you are ready to continue your journey. Finally, He is strong, and if He is, so are we. If He says keep going, then keep going with boldness. It does not matter where, when, how, what, or who; we have that faith that we are covered. There is no wasting time trying to figure anything out. He is our Tower, and nothing can knock Him down.

July 30

Define Family

Then he pointed to his disciples and said, "Look, these are my mother and brothers. Anyone who does the will of my Father in heaven is my brother and sister and mother!" (Matthew 12:49-50)

Yes, what does it mean to define family?

We each must ask who in our lives is a part of us? Who does life with you? Who knows you so well that they even know what you are going to say? Who knows your weaknesses, strengths, or insecurities and still is willing to be part of your life? Only those who genuinely love you, who stand with you, or share your beliefs (for some, this is important; for others, it may not be). Now please understand this. Our family is our biological family, unbelievers that are not yet ready to commit to God and believers. It is whoever does life with you, those who unconditionally love you, who give you grace, who understand and support you when there are no words. So, my family, God bless you and thank you for being part of my village in this journey to Jesus.

How Do We Stand?

Oh, the joys of those who do not follow the advice of the wicked, or stand around with sinners, or join in with mockers. (Psalm 1:1)

We should be standing in a specific posture (position of the body, in movement or at rest, or a mental or spiritual attitude), ready to leap forward to the next assignment that God puts in our hearts. We cannot support others who are not walking right with God or just standing, not going anywhere, but we can pray that God will help them reach our same path. Why? Because if we are not careful or lose sight of Jesus, we may lose our stance if we follow their bad habits. We should set our posture like we are in a ready position. We need others to be at that place with us. The verse says, "the joys of those that do not follow the advice of the wicked." Be leaders for Jesus, not standing still but holding your post and staying strong. Let others worry about their own but encourage them as well. Have a proper posture for God—on your knees, raised hands, or just looking up—and you will prosper.

August 1

Boldness with the Spirit

Stretch out your hand with healing power; may miraculous signs and wonders be done through the name of your holy servant Jesus." After this prayer, the meeting place shook, and they were all filled with the Holy Spirit. Then they preached the word of God with boldness. (Acts 4:30-31)

The Word says to stretch out our hands. It is a challenging thought, as we know sometimes we do not pray for others, but God says we must. So, I know for myself, I ask for forgiveness when I have not done that. We stretch out our hands for many things, such as holding, comforting someone in pain, and ensuring that they are not alone, just by putting our hands on their shoulders. Or even, just being hand-in-hand, locked tight, no words need to be said. That alone says it is okay to be weak because I will be decisive for us today. What do I mean? God expects us to stretch our hands out for Him to get to those who need His physical touch to know He is there; it is required, wanted, and comforting, especially for the ones in deep pain. I experienced it. "Thank you, God, that You use us like that." It is a moment between the one who needs, the one who is willing, and the ONE who will calm the storm. The rest and stillness for that moment are there. So, stretch out your hand for Jesus.

August 2

Refreshed Journey

The LORD has made everything for his own purposes, even the wicked for a day of disaster. (Proverbs 16:4)

God gave us free will, but He also promised that He will be with us and created us to live for Him until the end. Why continue wasting time? Why prolong our blessings by not choosing Him or following His commands? Struggles are real, but so is He. Reflect to see where you are in your journey. Are you temporarily stuck? Do you need to talk it out? Are you tired of seeking the world because it is draining, but you need a push in the right direction? Try to pinpoint where you are. Make a difference. Again, I say, if the ones you hang with are not helping you elevate in your journey with Jesus, then you might have to evaluate that. We, the creation, serve God's purpose to lead people to Him, not let others lead you to more of the world. Find you again. Do not worry about mistakes; He knows we will make them. He wants to fix our hearts, not break them.

August 3

Worthy Calling

Therefore I, a prisoner for serving the Lord, beg you to lead a life worthy of your calling, for you have been called by God. (Ephesians 4:1)

People lose themselves all the time. Things are removed from their lives because their identities were listening to others, following the world, or their jobs. What happened? But once God chooses you and leads you to your calling, that changes everything. You start to figure out who you are. The hardest part is the cost and sacrifice of time, focus, hardships, and isolation. Your circle gets smaller as others place a label on you or may not understand why God chose you (some accept, and others ignore). God must set boundaries. It may require you to step back from those that are not for you and hinder your calling. If you want to impact others, you must decide how necessary the calling is to you. To be called to live this worthy life is needed, but it is never easy. The journey will be lonely but rewarding.

August 4

20/20

I don't speak on my own authority. The Father who sent me has commanded me what to say and how to say it. And I know his commands lead to eternal life; so I say whatever the Father tells me to say." **(John 12:49-50)**

We need vision as we set on each of our missions: a clean slate and clear mind, pushing past people that do not understand what He is doing inside us. We feel awkward because we see ourselves walking, talking, and being this person we never thought we would be. The Holy Spirit led Jesus on what to say, think, or do. What does this mean to us? Do we understand this honor to be chosen and given the commandment to relay what He has placed in our hearts to help others? Some will take it; some will not understand and miss it because the world is so deeply ingrained inside them that it hinders their growth; some back away because they cannot handle letting go of their bad habits. Being chosen is not easy. People watch your steps as you represent Jesus. We must speak, walk, and live like Him as best as we can. Yes, loneliness will happen, but we have Him.

August 5

Your Prayers Heal

But the officer said, "Lord, I am not worthy to have you come into my home. Just say the word from where you are, and my servant will be healed. I know this because I am under the authority of my superior officers, and I have authority over my soldiers. I only need to say, 'Go,' and they go, or 'Come,' and they come. And if I say to my slaves, 'Do this,' they do it." (Matthew 8:8-9)

The faith of someone who loves you can help your healing process. Yes, God honors that and sees the faithful intervention of prayers until that person can stand again stronger than ever. But even the ones who pray and believe feel unworthy to be in God's presence. That is just how it is. We all have personal struggles. Take those struggles to the altar so your prayers can be effective. That is why our time with Him is so special: He reminds us we are His and loved. We do not have to be perfect to believe in Him. All He wants from us is to believe He can, even if it seems impossible. The Roman officer asked Jesus to say the word for his servant's healing because He knew when Jesus speaks, things change instantly. He rules all people, situations, or bondages.

August 6

Losing Changed to Blessing

Tell me, what have I done wrong? Show me my rebellion and my sin. (Job 13:23)

Every time something goes wrong, we try to figure out what we did wrong. We try to find justification for why or how it happened or focus on when something went wrong. In a test of faith, character, or patience, will we break or lean in closer? Job questioned why he was losing so much. He examined the pain and confusion that others put on him. He must have sinned; that was the only logical answer. But God allowed the test. Yes, we will get our consequences for purposely sinning, but God helps us develop our character under hardships. Will we trust or give up? Will we continue praising Him, believing in His promises, or will we crumble? Hold on to this: "this too shall pass." You will make it but stay under Jesus, not in the shadow of the world. Job was humbled and loved God. He did nothing wrong, but he passed and was blessed. He stayed faithful.

August 7

Zero Tolerance God

Make allowance for each other's faults, and forgive anyone who offends you. Remember, the Lord forgave you, so you must forgive others. (Colossians 3:13)

Sometimes it is hard to believe in someone you do not see. But it is also exciting to feel God's presence and see and believe in Him through daily living. You will see God in many things. But know God is direct. What He says not to do, we should not do. Why aren't we doing what He says to do, which will release so much within us? He gives us the strength to overcome any problem by showing us the risk and the reward. Continuing to tolerate the world will cause pain, making the battle harder to win because God does not accept what is not of Him. He reminds us to have tolerance for others, but live-in peace, be humble, forgive, and love, and this is what He approves. If we do not do this, then who is winning? Team Jesus is what we fight for and who we represent.

August 8

Between Us

You may believe there's nothing wrong with what you are doing, but keep it between yourself and God. Blessed are those who don't feel guilty for doing something they have decided is right. (Romans 14:22)

In our journey, we cannot worry about what others think. Are we worrying more about earthly thinking than our Eternal God? The verse says to keep our faith between ourselves and God. Yes, this is so important. No one knows you better than Him. This faith between you and God is unique. No one can compare to it: honest, genuine, unconditional, loving, safe, gives grace for those "I messed up" moments, and we never doubt this relationship at any moment as we do with earthly ones. Think of your relationship with Him. He knows we need physical beings to hold, to brainstorm our thoughts with, and with who we can love and do life with daily. Not everyone in our lives falls in this category, but they are out there. God blesses these relationships, as He is the first strand of the cord in them and needed in times of struggle. Pour more into God, and watch your faith rise.

Path Worth Stepping Into

Mark out a straight path for your feet; stay on the safe path. Don't get sidetracked; keep your feet from following evil. (Proverbs 4:26-27)

You know the choice is yours. Moving forward is not hard if you have Jesus directing your steps to places or into people's lives so that you can carry out what He created you to do. Now, yes, as you go forward, pillars may fall before you: confusion, family struggles, wondering who is on your team, anxiety about your path, questioning your new identity (not that it is terrible, but it is just unique and brings a peace within that you never knew, so it feels different). Keep going because you know wherever He leads you, it is good. But He will strip away what is unneeded because it must happen. Not everyone can handle where He is taking you, so let go if you can. But ask God to cover your heart. You get worse pillars if you follow the other path. Any path without Him will end up at a dead-end eventually. You will miss out, 100% guaranteed.

Keep Your Head Up

Then he asked them, "Why are you afraid? Do you still have no faith?" (Mark 4:40)

If you read before this verse, you will see it was about the disciples' faith and how they wanted Jesus to calm the storm at that moment instead of remaining calm and trusting that it would be okay. I am sure it was not easy. It was a fierce (vicious, intense, aggressive, dangerous, brutal) storm. The key is Jesus was in the boat with them, so why be afraid? Why are we fearful during our fierce storms? Human nature? Lack of faith? Fear of putting trust in someone we cannot see? Maybe. It depends on what each of us has in our boats on how we will respond. So be a Christian with a fierce attitude in the storms we face. Be on fire in your reading, studying, applying, and trusting Jesus's word, especially when you do not know. Remember, no giving up, no backing down, no "I can't, and only "I will." Stay focused and depend on the strength of Jesus, who is with us, who does not leave, and who calms those waves and storms around us.

True Family

Jesus replied, "My mother and my brothers are all those who hear God's word and obey it." (Luke 8:21)

Everyone wants to be a part of a family with shared beliefs and in a place of acceptance and love. Jesus had family and His followers. This verse shows how important His followers were to Him—just like us, we are also His family. Churches carry broken individuals and families. The impact that Jesus has on our hearts is so substantial that if anyone has ever felt misunderstood, unaccepted, judged, unloved, and continuously seeking approval, they seek refuge in Him. Jesus's house shows them they are loved, and this can be hard to understand for some. God knows what we lack in our families or who we lost (we will not be the same again), so what does He do? He provides those relationships we were seeking with our own families and gave us a new one: our church family. We love both, as they each pour into us differently. And because of this, families get healed, restored, and saved.

Dishonored

"But you dishonor my name with your actions. By bringing contemptible food, you are saying it's all right to defile the Lord's table. You say, 'It's too hard to serve the LORD,' and you turn up your noses at my commands," says the LORD of Heaven's Armies. "Think of it! Animals that are stolen and crippled and sick are being presented as offerings! Should I accept from you such offerings as these?" asks the LORD. (Malachi 1:12-13)

God pursues us daily, and if you look around your environment, you will see Him. But what we need to think about is our interactions with others can be difficult, absolutely, but there is a reason for that struggle. What am I saying? Being placed in an environment can build us, encourage us, educate us, and empower us. Our actions should encourage others to seek this God that has consumed our thoughts, hearts, and souls. Why do we give Him so much of us? We must be careful of our actions that can dishonor Him everywhere we go. Our actions speak so much volume to others. As soon as we accept Him, we make this covenant to stand beside Him and spread who He is—not only for them to know of Him but also to give them this HOPE or restore what discouraged them from following. We need to explore the cost of being who He wants and requires us to be in our actions.

August 13

Call Jesus

Seek the LORD while you can find him. Call on him now while he is near. (Isaiah 55:6)

God is always near us; we have to say His name. But we do have to understand what it says-seek while we can find Him. Will He always be there waiting for us to stop? We chase this world and regularly reject Him. We know how that feels not to be considered first choice or option B. God is not option B—let us keep that in mind. Some may think you cannot hear God speak, but He does as you read the Bible. You will listen to Him give you what you seek—clarity, direction, answers to difficult decisions are examples of what you will get. But go deeper seek His heart on how He unconditionally loves, forgives, and helps others so we can be like Him. Why is it hard to call for Him? But we have no problem calling for others that do not pour into our souls. No other name can guide us to eternity, peace, the tranquility of the heart, mind, and soul.

August 14

Only You, Jesus

Unless the LORD had helped me, I would soon have settled in the silence of the grave. I cried out, "I am slipping!" but your unfailing love, O LORD, supported me. (Psalm 94:17-18)

If Jesus is not in it, it is not worth the time, the mind, or the cost. Some may say, "but the world is so much more fun," "you are missing out," or "Jesus will always be there." Be careful with that thinking. Remember, if you are a Christian, we are not of this world. Yes, it entertains, but how is your soul level, faith level, or hope level? How does the world help you in your hardships? How does it comfort you? It may provide things that lessen the hurt, but only for a moment. God is waiting for you to stretch out your hand and grab His. So, no more struggles, no more wasting time, and no more trying to figure it out alone. Not one Christian can say, "I survived without Him." If you are confused, let this help your decision: "If God is in it, then this is what I want. If not, I do not want anything to do with it." Yes, it is that simple. His love will cover and support you with every step you take.

Stack Stones of Faith

"And so my judgment is that we should not make it difficult for the Gentiles who are turning to God. (Acts 15:19)

There are so many stumbling blocks that we need to avoid daily to stay focused on Jesus. People in the world might try to discourage us because their lives are not where they should be according to God's standards. It also might be how we are stuck on who we want to be versus who we need to be (something must break to move us further). It even might be trying to help others see who Jesus is, but as they hear you, the enemy speaks louder, and they step back. Our job is not to make it harder for others to come to Jesus. You may not see results immediately, but do not give up either. Step up louder in prayer so that stumbling blocks fall and our loved ones see Jesus. Praying and being there for them are the best weapons. Remind them that they are valued, not judged, and unconditionally loved. Always stand for what God created you to do, change stumbling blocks to stones of faith and trust. Who helped you gather your stones of faith?

August 16

A Woman after God's Own Heart

Don't be concerned about the outward beauty of fancy hairstyles, expensive jewelry, or beautiful clothes. You should clothe yourselves instead with the beauty that comes from within, the unfading beauty of a gentle and quiet spirit, which is so precious to God. (1 Peter 3:3-4)

Are we seeking His heart in singing, wor-shiping, reading verses, studying, and praying? What does He mean to you? This seeking will show how deep from the inside. Outward beauty is beautiful but what He is seeking is our true inner beauty, a gentle and quiet spirit going after God's heart that aims to be the woman that allows Him to lead and not fight against His will. It is trusting Him at all times, it is following Him even when we think we are sinking, and it is honoring Him with an unwavering and unchanging faith deep inside. It is genuinely repenting of our wrongs and following His right path at whatever cost, even if people walk away. Yes, our hearts will feel challenged as everyone will not understand why we seek Him or do what we do. Clothe with beauty within; this beauty grows stronger as we seek Him; others will see the truth by our speech and actions. Search your beauty within, and you will find His heart.

Dig Deeper for True Peace

"If you forgive those who sin against you, your heavenly Father will forgive you. But if you refuse to forgive others, your Father will not forgive your sins. (Matthew 6:14-15)

Digging unforgiveness out is not easy, but God is the only way we can accomplish it. The wound must open to find the core of your pain and pull it out with all attached to it, almost like a broken arrow piece that we do not want to take out because it hurts. We prefer to walk with the sting because it is the norm, but we are not free. But this is bigger: if we want to walk with God, we must genuinely forgive as He forgave us for our sins (which unforgiveness is one). Pulling from the core will bring tears, pain, and regrets. It is saying a final goodbye to whatever or whoever has held you back from finding healing. Yes, it is confronting the pain as it leaves your heart. But God and those He sends will be with us each moment of this process of healing.

August 18

Getting to Know God

Now we see things imperfectly, like puzzling reflections in a mirror, but then we will see everything with perfect clarity. All that I know now is partial and incomplete, but then I will know everything completely, just as God now knows me completely. (1 Corinthians 13:12)

We learn every day about our character but God's as well. As we get to know Him, we see His heart more clearly, but He still must tweak us, which can be challenging. Some parts fit together, and some do not. If they do, then the puzzle is created. The same is valid for being a follower of Jesus: if we put the puzzle pieces together, our purpose has started. These pieces include being obedient, loving others, accepting others, helping others, reading the Word, and applying what you learn from others who have the wisdom or learning beside you. The best pieces of the puzzle are peace, serenity, and tranquility. The person God made you to be will have more parts of the puzzle added until completion. If the pieces (people or situations) do not fit, they are not suitable for us. Why force them? Only God controls the completed picture of the puzzle.

August 19

Evaluation Day

"Understand this: If a homeowner knew exactly when a burglar was coming, he would not permit his house to be broken into. You also must be ready all the time, for the Son of Man will come when least expected." (Luke 12:39-40)

This verse will cause uneasiness depending on where you are at on your journey. Are you ready for Jesus if He were to come today? Some may say yes—until the day they see Him. Then they regret what they should have done when He knocked on the door (the door opens, but they only let Him halfway in). He is the answer to all struggles. Yes, we need Jesus to come in as the horror of this world can be so overwhelming, and it can consume every thought in our minds; this can even cause us to create two mindsets: the world and Jesus. Let us ask Jesus to help us restructure our Godly mindset, just as you had before, as we must be ready when He comes. Jesus knows we are not perfect and must see that He is our only choice without wavering. What will you say to Him when He is before you? Will you cry of relief and gratitude from the cost He endured? Will you get the answers you have been seeking from Him personally?

Again

Whenever the LORD raised up a judge over Israel, he was with that judge and rescued the people from their enemies throughout the judge's lifetime. For the LORD took pity on his people, who were burdened by oppression and suffering. (Judges 2:18)

We know the Israelites': God would put someone over them, then when that person was removed or passed away, they went back to their old ways until the next time. Does this sound familiar? Yes, going back to your old ways feels comfortable, but wouldn't you instead feel uncomfortable, in a new way, living with Jesus? In this verse, God feels sad about what His people were going through when their lives could have been better if they were obedient. Our actions fall on us if we know who we are in this journey and still choose to be disobedient. The world makes everything attainable, and it might feel right at the moment—until reality hits. We have a void inside us that feels empty, but only Jesus can fill it. Our God lets us sting for a bit to learn a lesson, but He is the first to pick us up and push us to fly again. Jesus must be the core of our being.

August 21

Promises are True

No, I will not break my covenant; I will not take back a single word I said. (Psalm 89:34)

As you seek God, you will find your prayers answered by God's promise that He will not hold anything from us that is good and that will align with His will. He will not take a word back. Sometimes that is a hard pill to swallow. Things around us consume our minds in some moments, and everything seems to fall apart, but then we read this verse. When our faith comes in, and we either trust Him, or we do not. Not one promise will fail us. So, when you do hear the voice of God, know it is accurate, and when you listen to the voice of the enemy trying to confuse you, think otherwise, then pray against it. If God said, He would be with us, we believe it. If He says have the faith of a mustard seed, then have that faith. If He says do not fear and stand firm, we need to look up and do it. Yes, I know it is not accessible during hardships, but our hope must be beyond what we can imagine, believe, or even feel. How can it be that He loves us so much?

August 22

Image Made

So God created human beings in his own image. In the image of God he created them; male and female he created them. (Genesis 1:27)

If we are entertaining this world and its image, know that it is not part of God's image, which may be the reason for our daily struggles. Nothing can be imperfect in His image because that is not what He represents. To have been created in such a way gives us a purpose, and all we need to fulfill it is Him. We struggle, right? I know it is just human nature, but that is the mindset of a worldly image, not God's. What God creates is perfect, good, strong, unshakable, and unbreakable, but it is not His fault that we make decisions that break us, shake us, cause us to lose sight of His plan, and that does not allow us even to attempt to be the best we can be. No one will ever be perfect like God but having the image of God means we represent the best of who He is—in our speech and our actions. It is serious business. It is not easy for us, as the tug-of-war between our wants and God's expectations is a genuine struggle.

Will You be Fruitful or Fruitless?

Then God blessed them and said, "Be fruitful and multiply. Fill the earth and govern it. Reign over the fish in the sea, the birds in the sky, and all the animals that scurry along the ground." (Genesis 1:28)

God said it, be fruitful and multiply. Spreading the word of God should not be a problem, but why are so many lost in this world? Can we not reach out to spread the truth, or are people not interested because of the cost? The same way someone poured into you is how we need to reach others, to let them know there is a place at the table for them just as they are. We need to walk in the authority that we have so we can multiply. I pray we all get an opportunity to share who Jesus is, the Hope to the hopeless, the Comforter to all who mourn (not only death but sins of the past that still haunt the heart and get in the way of growth), and the True love of our lives. We all have the gift to attract others with who we are— without judgment, with a smile, a hug, a shared word, or just being present. One person at a time, we can make a difference in God's Kingdom.

Hidden

Truly, O God of Israel, our Savior, you work in mysterious ways. (Isaiah 45:15)

If we ever think God is not working, then maybe we need to check ourselves. That is the beauty of chasing a God that we cannot see but yet performs miracles, heals, and makes impossible situations possible. He works mysteriously in His timing, in His way, and His children for His will. Is that what keeps us running after Him? Or is it just because we know He loves us, is for us and is with us? The answer is all of it and more. No one can ever love us more than Him, sacrifice for us as He did, or fix all our problems like He can because He is the only Creator who can know His creation's needs and wants. We need to trust in His timing and His mysterious ways. We need to trust that He knows how things in our lives will work out. I cannot say it will be easy because it is not. But I will say that He will direct us, give us the patience to wait for His answers, and show us how to trust Him.

August 25

To Live

The man answered, "'You must love the LORD your God with all your heart, all your soul, all your strength, and all your mind.' And, 'Love your neighbor as yourself.'" (Luke 10:27)

We are to love with all that we are: with our mind, strength, and heart. To love is to allow others in, knowing and risking the heart and all attached to it. Some do not give the same love back with truth, honesty, or loyalty, but what do we do? Yes, we try our best to do what God expects from us, and He takes care of the rest. You may have tears, but someday He will show you why you shed them. Hear this, love yourself, and trust in yourself. That peace you feel is the Spirit when you pour out all you can in love, time, talent, or just being the best you can. Guess what. YOU are enough. The only being that defines you is Jesus, so whatever or whoever tries to hurt your character, pray against it. You have to have faith that you have a purpose, and you are part of a change in His Kingdom. So, no more stopping, just running with all that you are and with Jesus's love overflowing. I say you are already winning.

Quietness for God

You faithfully answer our prayers with awesome deeds, O God our savior. You are the hope of everyone on earth, even those who sail on distant seas. (Psalm 65:5)

Yes, I can hear some of the responses already. Some do not like to wait, but sometimes if we listen, God is protecting us from the damage others can do and the damage we can do to ourselves. It is not easy, as anxious thoughts and hopeless feelings can discourage us from holding on. Injustices against us are not easy to wait through for God to address. But if we say God is our hope, trust, faith, or defender, then we must continue seeking His ways and fighting the enemy as he tries to convince us that God does not care. Our prayer to God should be to help us wait patiently—even if it hurts us—for the best answer, and if He takes away, we love even more. In waiting, we learn that He is in control. We must endure in those moments because we trust Him, and that makes it all worth it. A true believer understands this and does not run or give up.

August 27

Love Will Drive You

"I love all who love me. Those who search will surely find me. (Proverbs 8:17)

Okay, I cannot stress enough that our journey is like a race to Jesus. It does not matter how fast, slow, or who you pass. Just get to Him. Then turn around and cheer the ones you passed. Even if you are the last person, do not give up and do not get discouraged. Still know Jesus is waiting. Stay focused, run with diligence (persistence and effort) to find Jesus's love, not letting the world impede what He has for us. The Word says, "He loves all who love Him." Why are we searching this world in places, gathering with people, or things we know He will never be around? Why do we waste our time? Yes, we search for sites that we know He is against because it does not bring life but rather gently pulls us away. Yes, we search for people who do not elevate us. Now it is okay to be with others if you show or pour out His love with your words and actions. We are to help those who do not know and show He truly exists. But in all that you seek, make sure He is present there.

Saying Goodbye

Examine yourselves to see if your faith is genuine. Test yourselves. Surely you know that Jesus Christ is among you; if not, you have failed the test of genuine faith. (2 Corinthians 13:5)

We are to examine ourselves to see where our faith is because we walk with the Spirit. What does that mean? Knowing that within us is this being that we wanted, searched for, and relied on to get from point A to point B, we still set the Holy Spirit aside so that we can rule our world. Yet when the world knocks us down, we plead to the Spirit, "Help us." What do we want? Revenge? To see those who hurt us suffer? Is that Jesus? Listen to the Spirit, pray without giving up, seek His will, put down your selfish ways, and pick up the original method. If bitterness, anger, and resentment are your driving force—even though we have justifications in our minds—how does your life have peace? These emotions will tear us apart. Be vulnerable without caring about who is watching. It feels weird, but it is called peace and trust in Jesus. We must pass the test of faith, not the test of fear. Release: it is a mindset we choose; no one has power over us but God.

Who Is Watching Out for You?

He took Peter and Zebedee's two sons, James and John, and he became anguished and distressed. He told them, "My soul is crushed with grief to the point of death. Stay here and keep watch with me." (Matthew 26:37-38)

It is hard to fix our crushed soul when things happen to us—health issues, loss of someone we cared about, our struggles with God's expectations, and our expectations. The tug-of-war within is why we need God to help us, and we need others to pray for us. We need others to watch out for us when we cannot think straight or need that little help, to pray with us in unity and strength. Jesus did not ask others to walk with Him on His journey to the cross. He was walking in solitude with God, but when He needed that spiritual lift from others—as He knew what He had to go through for us to live—they did not show up. I pray that the ones you trust show up for you and take it seriously when you need spiritual help. He struggled too, was human, but He overcame because He had to finish the will of God. We need to end well with His will accomplished. Keep going, Overcomers.

Weakness Turns to Meekness

God blesses those who are humble, for they will inherit the whole earth. (Matthew 5:5)

Jesus walked with meekness, which is strength under control and maintaining peace during confrontations. Some of us can walk in humility, but some do not have the patience or compassion to understand that we cannot help others if we do not. We will encounter people on our journey who God brings our way, but they come with various hurts, anger, or brokenness. Therefore, those walls have a hard time coming down. When someone gives unconditional love to them, they may not know how to accept it, so they pull away instead of embracing it. He does not want to break us, but He wants to make us better for His purpose, especially when His plan for some of us involves leadership roles. Jesus changed many with His humility, and He never judged. The Spirit will help you to walk in humility and obedience.

Always Seek His Favor

Never let loyalty and kindness leave you! Tie them around your neck as a reminder. Write them deep within your heart. Then you will find favor with both God and people, and you will earn a good reputation. (Proverbs 3:3-4)

Everyone has a story or testimony to tell. Our testimonies should help us stay loyal, humble, faithful, and kind because we were at our worst when we found God. I do not know about you, but I never want to go back to where I was before I met Jesus (yeah, He got me at hello). Once you are in the Word, a fierce fire is ignited inside you to keep going continuously. The world does such an excellent job of blinding us to the wonders of what God has for us. We are to do all that we can to be the best representation of God's love using these daily reminders to ourselves. You know what to do. Why wait another minute not receiving His blessings? His favor is what we seek and accept when we do what He commands, and through this, others will see through your obedience that God is real. Do right. Be right. And you will see right.

He is Your Answer

"So remember this and keep it firmly in mind: The LORD is God both in heaven and on earth, and there is no other. If you obey all the decrees and commands I am giving you today, all will be well with you and your children. I am giving you these instructions so you will enjoy a long life in the land the LORD your God is giving you for all time." (Deuteronomy 4:39-40)

We search for what will give us freedom from what aches inside, from our bondages, for what gives answers, or for someone to lead us to where we must go for peace of mind in all areas of our lives. The Israelites were reminded never to forget what God did for them, but they had a cycle of disobedience that a return to God would follow. Then repeat. Just as Moses reminds them, we should also. It says all will be well with you and your children, but I pray that you see that this extends to all who are attached to us if we are faithful to His commands and believe that He is who He says He is. There is no other like Him. The verse says, "keep it firmly in mind." So here it goes: stay focused, encouraged, prayed up, and believe in our omnipresent God. Surrender everything, knowing He will take care of it at His time, not ours.

September 2

Watch What You Say or Do?

A good person produces good things from the treasury of a good heart, and an evil person produces evil things from the treasury of an evil heart. (Matthew 12:35)

This verse is about good versus bad. We all know a good heart poured out to others will produce good things. It shows in how we talk, act, or walk. Why not remain with a good spirit instead of letting our defenses come up to win a battle that does not matter? You know how it goes: if you entertain bad things, you will let evil into your heart and not produce anything good. Remember to ask yourself, where is God in this? Anything without God will never succeed. We can try faking it, but those who know God will see through it. These people are interceding in prayer for anyone struggling. Jesus knows the heart of the struggle and how it continually tries to be good yet likes some of the bad, too. But the bad will cost you your salvation, your relationship with Him and others, your identity, and your opportunity to know and feel His heart of love. The good spirits of Jesus never stop praying for those who gave theirs to the enemy.

September 3

A Saved Soul

But we are not like those who turn away from God to their own destruction. We are the faithful ones, whose souls will be saved. (Hebrews 10:39)

"Thank you, Jesus, for all the souls that were so lost, but you saved." Sadness comes when you see people who still follow that wide path, knowing there is a God but do not want to go through the cost of following Him on the narrow path. Honestly, it is true: we cannot do anything for them but pray, let go, or step back and let God. Everyone has a choice to make during suffering: either we will crumble, like the world, with no peace, or stand in position with faith in a God we cannot see but who provides us this peace and courage to keep going. If you read before this verse, it says God does not take pleasure from those who turn away, so PRAY for those on that broad path of destruction. God will flip it if they genuinely repent. One soul saved at a time, penetrating their hearts to the point that all they can say is "Jesus." They will be brought back stronger than ever in a grounded, unwavering FAITH.

God Gives a New Song

He has given me a new song to sing, a hymn of praise to our God. Many will see what he has done and be amazed. They will put their trust in the LORD. (Psalm 40:3)

Constant thinking sometimes makes us feel like we cannot breathe for a moment. Other times, when our cup is overflowing, we want to run up the highest mountain, be in His presence, and sing. The verse says He has given us a new song to sing because we were lost and now found, vulnerable and now victorious, broken and now restored. I think you get what I am trying to say. Lyrics of songs change because they do not sound good or a word is not clicking, so you must rewrite it to make sense, have meaning, and impact others. Apply it to your life: God must give us a new song (energy) because the one we have been singing does not work due to all those lyrics of struggle. Music worn-out means its lyrics have no meaning without God, or it does not impact others. Let God rewrite your song because others are waiting to listen and need YOU.

September 5

Remember Them

Remember your leaders who taught you the word of God. Think of all the good that has come from their lives, and follow the example of their faith. (Hebrews 13:7)

I always tell those who have walked with me and poured into me how grateful I am that they took the time—a walk, a talk, a word of wisdom, a cry, or hold with no comments—to support and encourage me. You see, God knows who can handle us. A good leader leads, teaches, listens, and shows by example and must keep it real by challenging those they lead. Transparency is not an easy position for anyone to be in, but it must show you have humbly overcome because of Jesus alone. Leaders go through and endure life's challenges, but they press forward, as they know that God has a purpose for them and all who follow them; this drives leaders even more to witness the transformation of lives. Growth and fruit should come from their influence, not bad seeds. If that is your case, pray for God to change them. The enemy will attack them more but will not succeed, as they are untouchable, walking with God's covering.

Stop Withdrawing What God has Deposited

By his divine power, God has given us everything we need for living a godly life. We have received all of this by coming to know him, the one who called us to himself by means of his marvelous glory and excellence. (2 Peter 1:3)

We all work to maintain relationships, jobs, self-care or raise others, never to give up. The force of this world is brutal, but the power of our God is stronger. Everything we need to get through life He put in us. So, let us think about this: what He put in us is good, so why do we keep wasting time on worldly nonsense instead of just growing stronger in what we have (Jesus)? It is so important to wake up to this. Not many will enter the narrow path because they believe Jesus somehow was not enough? Can we keep it real? Could this be our thinking sometimes? Our faith will show by our actions. Be careful not to misrepresent Jesus, as we are responsible for those who Jesus sends our way. Our job is to help others get into the boat, not keep drowning in their confusion. Sometimes we do not show there is a different way. Withdrawing will cause us to struggle with our God-given identity.

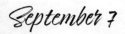

September 7

For the Least

"And the King will say, 'I tell you the truth, when you did it to one of the least of these my brothers and sisters, you were doing it to me!' (Matthew 25:40)

It can be challenging to be that strength for those who struggle to defend themselves or are helpless and depend on others. Our emotions go up in the air. The one who must help will adjust patience, understanding, and unconditional love. Some are vulnerable due to mental or physical illness. Why can't others consider their feelings as they don't like to rely on others or sometimes misunderstood because of their fears, confusions, pressures, and worries? God flips it when He gives us the power to do things for others because we do it for Him (forgive us if we fail in these areas, we should have had more compassion). We are His hands and feet. His words should come out of our mouths to uplift others. Jesus gives us His strength, as life can wear us down—it just does; no sugar coating, it is hard—but God guides us the whole way. Step back under His wings, recharge, and keep going.

With Him or Not?

"Anyone who isn't with me opposes me, and anyone who isn't working with me is actually working against me. (Matthew 12:30)

The truth is if we are not with Jesus, then we are against Him. We not only have to be Jesus to others, but we must activate everything He represents. Who do you thank for the blessings you have; do you say, "Thank you, enemy?" Or when hardships come, do you say, "Help me enjoy" or "Thank you for tripping me up again?" What does it take to completely capture your heart to the point where you do not sway to the left (world)? Find your balance in Him. Do not end up regretting missing out on the blessings that are waiting for you. To know Him, we must be with Him—that is TRUTH. If not, you will not feel Him; get to know Him for who He is or experience what He can do for you and your loved ones. Old ways keep us stuck. You will never find that true peace or contentment you seek. We can try to fake it but not with God. The enemy takes more and more, and it will just be more work for Jesus to pull us back. But He wins at the end. Do not keep losing the ones who genuinely love you because of this world.

No Need to Take Cover

He guards the paths of the just and protects those who are faithful to him. (Proverbs 2:8)

There is such a feeling of peace when we truly and genuinely seek Jesus, who gives so much of himself to us and true wisdom comes from Him. First, always go to the Bible if you are ever in doubt. You probably know that He guards (protects against damage or harm) us wherever we go, but we must keep that covenant that we have with Him. Sometimes things can shake us on our path. It just happens; that is life. But we always have two options: give up or keep going on that path. To know God is to stop, give Him glory, and say, "Please lead us. This path is getting a little rocky. We need your covering for our thoughts, for what we hear, for what we see and feel." God protects the heart with peace that helps you to get back on track. Rocky moments will always come our way, but we stand on our Rock, who keeps us standing firm and unshakable.

Will You Walk with Courage or Will You Crumble?

When doubts filled my mind, your comfort gave me renewed hope and cheer. (Psalm 94:19)

If you are in tune with God, fear has no place in you, above you, or around you. Fear, anxiety, or depression cannot take over the space in your mind or heart that belongs to God. It can try pressing you down, but the word of God says His comfort gives renewed hope in moments of doubt. I practice this when those moments come. I claim it in Jesus's name—whatever it is—and say, "You got to go. You (whatever is troubling me at that moment) have no place in my mind; this space belongs to Jesus." You know the journey: when you have been searching so long for what you feel you lack, you find Jesus and feel completely content. Why would we risk losing Him? Fight the battle with all you got. Despite whatever is trying to pull you down or overwhelm you, do not cave in, give up, or negotiate it. Crumbling is not an option, but courageous steps forward are. His words shake off anything, not of Him.

What Are Your Parables?

Once again Jesus began teaching by the lakeshore. A very large crowd soon gathered around him, so he got into a boat. Then he sat in the boat while all the people remained on the shore. (Mark 4:1)

Jesus always told parables that showed a moral or spiritual lesson to teach His followers. Parables may be confusing at first, but they are stories using daily living people or things (mustard seed, lamp, etc.) to communicate a more meaningful message. Were these things relatable? Yes, because people could connect at any level of understanding. Jesus meets us at all levels. So here it goes: we encounter people daily and connect with them. Tell them your faithful parables if it helps, so people can better understand this spiritual journey you are on. If we teach, present, and speak in ways that capture hearts from our stories, those on the receiving end will share their own stories.

September 12

True Confession–Healed

Confess your sins to each other and pray for each other so that you may be healed. The earnest prayer of a righteous person has great power and produces wonderful results. (James 5:16)

A confession admits your wrong in action or thought against God; this is the first step in healing. We are all guilty. It is not easy when we reveal the truth, but it is healing. Sometimes you get more respect for being honest than for sugar coating your life. Prayers in unity and sincerity break the control any bondages have over us that slow us down— whether physical, emotional, or mental. It is okay not to be okay, but just for a moment. Then we must put on the protective vest of Jesus and keep going. The verse states that the righteous have great power and produce beautiful results. So, if we are not right in this area, how can we create the good works God expects of us? Pray for each other, and watch healing happen.

September 13

Help Wanted

When he saw the crowds, he had compassion on them because they were confused and helpless, like sheep without a shepherd. (Matthew 9:36)

The job Jesus assigns is to help Him gather the ones who are helpless or lost. With no direction, where will they go? Jesus was and is always at work, still loves, and always has compassion. When He sees daily His creation struggle, how can't it hurt? He sees the lost, broken, or confused, and He is all-knowing and all-powerful and wants us to partner with Him. But make sure that you feel willing and generous, not obligated. You will walk with His heart, not your own. You will have the compassionate mindset to withhold judgment. Everyone does not start the journey in the same manner, so we should always be sensitive. God knows you and who you will attract if you allow the Spirit to lead. We help save souls—which is the goal—one by one. More workers mean more commitment, prayers, interceding, patience, and overflowing of Jesus. Will you apply for the job?

September 14

Restructured Character

Remember how the LORD your God led you through the wilderness for these forty years, humbling you and testing you to prove your character, and to find out whether or not you would obey his commands. (Deuteronomy 8:2)

Our wilderness experience is where we learn to trust God, accepting what He will pour into us during that time. God will put our character in a test mode. How do you know? Well, when you are soaking in Jesus all you can, things from our past come our way. We thought we overcame that now comes to tempt us, but we must make sure we step back and ask God to reveal it clearly and help us get through it. We must pass the test. He will see if you are genuinely for Him or just acting. God wants to see where our morals (right or wrong) stand; this must be clear in our journeys. We must always choose what is right in God's eyes. It is not easy, as our hurt will cause us to want to go through the easy route, but where does this lead? Be humble and make the best decisions you can make. Any right decision will leave you with a peace that no one understands but you.

He Will

The LORD says, "I will rescue those who love me. I will protect those who trust in my name. When they call on me, I will answer; I will be with them in trouble. I will rescue and honor them. I will reward them with a long life and give them my salvation." (Psalm 91:14-16)

We hold on to Jesus when difficult times come our way. Just as He says, He will rescue us from dangerous or distressing (causing anxiety, sorrow, pain, or upsetting) situations. I do not know what we expect, but knowing this causes excitement, joy, happiness, or strong confidence standing in His presence. But sometimes—this is what we cannot forget—when that bulldozer (troubles that try to distract your faith by targeting your emotions or peace in Him) comes your way, which you did not expect. I have not counted, but God says, "I will" a lot in the Bible. It is comforting when I hear Him say that because I know that I meet the requirement of being rescued and protected by Him. I love and trust Him with everything I have. I place it all in His hands, and I know you do too. All that God promises is what we need to remember and hold on to during challenging times.

September 16

Show Me More of You

If it is true that you look favorably on me, let me know your ways so I may understand you more fully and continue to enjoy your favor. And remember that this nation is your very own people." (Exodus 33:13)

God chose Moses to lead His people to the Promised Land. His relationship with God was close. If you read before this verse, it says that He spoke to Moses as a friend. He was favored but always needed the assurance of God's presence. Does anyone ever need that? To know God is in it with you, that He sees you, that He hears you or cries with you? Moses wanted to learn more about God to have a better understanding of His ways. To understand God, you must seek Him. That is the key to knowing what He expects from us. Some of His ways we may understand, but some we will not ever understand. Every moment we spend seeking Him is not wasted time, but it is a wasted life if we invest in this world. You see, Moses knew God and what He had done for him but still wanted more understanding of Him. God gives it bit by bit to see how we will handle it. So, trust, and God will reveal to you what you need to know. But be ready to move.

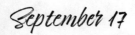

September 17

Unexplainable Love

We know how much God loves us, and we have put our trust in his love. God is love, and all who live in love live in God, and God lives in them. (1 John 4:16)

Unless someone knows and experiences God's love, they cannot say they love truthfully. Be careful. The One who gives love is Jesus, so we need to know Him and walk with this love within us to pour it out to others. As the verse says, all who live in God live in love. May you know that God's love is unconditional and available every minute of the day. His love will always be what we can count on, put our hope in, and stand on the foundation of truth. If you are searching for true love, then find Jesus. Loving is not easy. That is why we need God's heart of love to help us forgive, understand, or choose battles with others. It is not about what they think; it is about who we are or want to be in Jesus. YOU are loved and accepted just the way you are, and most importantly, Jesus loves you.

September 18

A Sadden God

Jesus continued, "You are from below; I am from above. You belong to this world; I do not. That is why I said that you will die in your sins; for unless you believe that I AM who I claim to be, you will die in your sins." (John 8:23-24)

Who would not be sad if they sacrificed for someone to help them find their way and loved unconditionally? Jesus is a relational God. What does that mean? All He wants is to help us, for us to believe in Him and His truth (but He does not force), to grow us, love us, bless us, encourage us to seek the things He wants us to, such as the lost souls. Does anyone know anyone lost right now—that still stuck on neutral—not sure if this Christian walk is right for them or the present worldly time? There is no comparison of who has our best interest; yes, if we want destruction in who we are – we will find it in this world. Jesus walked to be with all those people, who had all different situations and with what we read all were touched one way or another by a word, a touch, or a story—may we do the same for others, may we remember why we are here, so we do not keep ignoring a God with so much heart.

Devoted Thankfulness

Devote yourselves to prayer with an alert mind and a thankful heart. (Colossians 4:2)

It should not be hard to be thankful for what God has done and will continue to do. We share all that we are grateful for on Thanksgiving, but do we carry those thoughts daily in our hearts? Or is it just in the moment? Let us go deeper: Jesus gives us grace and helps us to love with genuine compassion, He allows us to love those with imperfection, those who love us with our weaknesses, for moments of silliness and laughter, for moments of solitude in His presence, for just being ourselves and knowing He hears and sees us. That He chooses each of us to accomplish a purpose and to help others find their way back to Him or find Him, so ponder on what moves you. Keep praying in all situations. Be thankful that you do not have to understand because He does. Watch Him show you how strong you are. Thank Him for His peace, calmness, healing, and love.

September 20

Dry Bones

The LORD took hold of me, and I was carried away by the Spirit of the LORD to a valley filled with bones. (Ezekiel 37:1)

What does it mean to be at a place of dry

bones? For some, it can be a time of stagnancy, of wanting to move but the heaviness of life is keeping you down. It can feel like no spiritual direction, having lost hope because you have allowed your light (Jesus) to dim a little and lose focus. Flip it: as you read the verse, it says the Lord took hold of me (thank you, Jesus; my daily prayer to Jesus is never let me go, which I pray the same for you). To lose the grip of Jesus is to lose ourselves. Some may think they can do it alone, but they struggle and are just trying to survive. They walk in circles only to end up in the same place, with minimal hope versus an overflow of hope. Also, the verse says that the Spirit of the Lord carries Ezekiel. Let Him lead you today to where you are going on your journey, and may you find comfort knowing that in the most challenging moments, He has always had you. Just let go.

Finish the Race is the Goal

I have fought the good fight, I have finished the race, and I have remained faithful. (2 Timothy 4:7)

To run a race, you must train your body to endure the distance. If not, you will not go far. The same is true for our walk with Jesus; we must train to be fit enough to carry out His will. What do I mean? Practice pull-ups by holding others and standing together to show that the other is their strength when one is weak. Strengthen your legs and feet by walking the bumpy journey and by jumping over life's hurdles. Dancing will pump up your heart by sharing Jesus and loving unconditionally to strengthen you in times of suffering (yes, this is part of it, but God has us— all tears He has in His hands). Meditate to improve your mind by being still, resting your thoughts to think, ponder, plan the next move when the enemy throws you a curveball and remaining calm to hear God say: "I'm here; I got you; we have to get through this." You get the picture. We need to train our souls to be strong, healthy, prepared and maintained to do His work for the long haul.

A Joyous Moment

So you have sorrow now, but I will see you again; then you will rejoice, and no one can rob you of that joy. (John 16:22)

I am not sure about you, but I picture the day I see Jesus to be a beautiful moment. Here in this verse, He tells the disciples that although they will be sad for a while, a time will come when He comes back, and they will rejoice. Being with Him again will be a moment for them that no one can take away. The same is true for us now: we live with the Holy Spirit within us and walk with the Trinity. Who can take that away from us? Why do we allow others to take the joy away from us? Or do we lay our pleasures down in compromise, to have relationships with people who do not have what we have inside? We must hold on to that overflowing feeling of anticipation that Jesus is with us daily, that He saved us, walks before us, healed areas that no other could, that He loved us so much that He sacrificed everything for us. Who else would do this? Yeah, this joy we carry will overflow when we see Him. Hold onto it tight, especially when tough times come.

Hope Was Born

I pray that God, the source of hope, will fill you completely with joy and peace because you trust in him. Then you will overflow with confident hope through the power of the Holy Spirit. (Romans 15:13)

Be hopeful, not hopeless. In all of our journeys, there is hope. Yes, even in those dark moments. In a world of busyness, bitterness, confusion, faithlessness, and struggles, He came to save and help us from further damage and to protect us from the enemy. I once saw a pamphlet with the numbers 3:16. Yes, *"For this is how God loved the world: He gave his one and only Son, so that everyone who believes in him will not perish but have eternal life"* (John 3:16). The one and only Son would bring eternal life. He did not come to make us feel defeated (the enemy does this daily when the armor does not cover us). Love unconditionally, walk peacefully, be joyful, and step into His hope. Hope is pressing forward, trusting His ways, and walking confidently in the belief that He is for us every day.

This is How We Fight Our Battles

He will cover you with his feathers. He will shelter you with his wings. His faithful promises are your armor and protection. (Psalm 91:4)

What more can we ask other than this C.S.P (covered, sheltered, and promises)? There will be times when what we have on our plates can discourage us or make us feel like we are losing the battles. But then God says to us, "Step back under my coverage; rest yourself, breathe, and let's look at other options on how to get through this one." Thank God for our physical shelters, but there is something about God's protection that provides hope inside that reminds us that we can stay in His presence and do not have to leave until we feel safe. Yeah, there is nothing better than those moments. Remember this: implant scripture into your heart because those are His promises that guarantee the good for our lives. We also need to use the full armor to combat and protect us from the enemy's schemes. Relying on our strength and words will make us lose even more because only God's word wins battles. We need to believe in Him.

September 25

What is Placed in Your Heart?

Dear children, keep away from anything that might take God's place in your hearts. (1 John 5:21)

I shared with some of my sisters that nothing else can take His place whenever God is in your mind or heart. What we allow to occupy our hearts and minds is what will control us. God warns us to stay away from anything not of Him because He knows the weakness of the flesh. He knows we will break and regret our mistakes later. Why? Okay, I know that our flesh is weak, but get out of it as soon as you feel it pulling you away from God's heart. Anything that pulls us away from God will lead to confusion, which leads to personal identity issues. Then who do we blame? God always warns us, but are we truly listening? Maybe it is easier to be in worldly things than in our spiritual walk; can this be our thinking? How is your heart, truthfully? Be real. Is it broken because you lost your way and did not know how to stand up—left confused, angry, bitter, or judged? Prayer is what we need for restored hearts because fake ones do not ever get healed.

Every Moment Recorded

You saw me before I was born. Every day of my life was recorded in your book. Every moment was laid out before a single day had passed. (Psalm 139:16)

As you look at footprints, imagine them as a symbol of our lives: all the times we have been at crossroads, coming or going leaves one set of prints. We walk or act on our own until we see we align with God's steps, then we finally let Him carry us or direct us where to go or to whom. The best part is that we are never alone in the various stages of our lives. Sometimes those steps took us in a direction that we needed to travel to learn that our path ends nowhere without Him. Allow Him to lead you. No more wasted time going down the wrong direction as you figure out your path. We may never fit right in His footsteps—as He is perfect—but follow Him, even if you do not know where it will lead. We do know that wherever He leads, we are safe, we learn from it, and we teach others down the same path (or walk together side-by-side). Yeah, follow the Leader. Walk each grounded, faithful step with God.

September 27

God Grants

He was the one who prayed to the God of Israel, "Oh, that you would bless me and expand my territory! Please be with me in all that I do, and keep me from all trouble and pain!" And God granted him his request. (1 Chronicles 4:10)

We all want to be blessed by God and have His hands in all we do, mainly to keep us from evil. It also states not causing any pain to anyone (some do without realizing it, so keep those in prayer, most importantly, we must make sure we are not the initiator of it). Blessings come in many ways, but the one we should want the most is the one of peace in His presence, contentment, and just being loved. If God's hands are in all we d—we must pray to Him, trust His answers, and know if He is in it—what is there to worry about, even in hard decisions that need to have an answer. God will grant a prayer if it is aligned with His Kingdom and will, so maybe we should think about our motives before lifting a prayer that does not have His best interest because He has our interest daily. I pray today He grants your prayers, shows up, and keeps you safe.

September 28

Just Walk

And so I walk in the LORD's presence as I live here on earth! (Psalm 116:9)

We realize that we had losses, break-throughs, discovery of self again, and life challenges every day. There is no getting around this: we endure. The enemy is always trying to knock us off track on our journey, but we survive. It is not easy to stand firm during struggles. Some people throw in the towel. If that is you, it is not to make you feel guilty. I want to remind you to get back on this journey because you are loved, needed to help others, and have a purpose. We always win with God. We must press through, endure the test of faith, and show God what He put in us is activated and not broken. We must defend ourselves from anything the enemy throws at us. Our God wins all battles, so we win, too. Be bold and know that He directs you. If God is not in it, do not move until you see His presence. Pray, read, trust, love, hope, believe, and be you. Forgive, and place it all in His hands. Then you can walk in His peace.

Change

For I am about to do something new. See, I have already begun! Do you not see it? I will make a pathway through the wilderness. I will create rivers in the dry wasteland. (Isaiah 43:19)

If we want a new thing, then we must allow God to help us. Sometimes I believe He watches to see if we will follow where He is directing us or continue struggling because of selfishness. If we want to change, He is the only One who can help. Why? Because it is not easy alone, especially if we are emotionally attached to people or things that we know are not helping us on this journey. Understand that we can pray for them, but if He says to step back or you will not see the changes of good I have for you, then you lose out if you do not listen. Do you want God's favor, or do you want worldly failure? Do you want faith or fear? In your journey with Him, the ride will still be bumpy, but you will ride with Him through these moments. As the verse says, He will make a way in the wilderness. Has He not shown us already? Change if you want peace and favor. Let go of what holds you down (it will hurt), especially if God tells you. We do not lose with Him by our side.

Angels All Around

For he will order his angels to protect you wherever you go. (Psalm 91:11)

An angel is a human or superhuman agent or messenger of God. God always sends them to protect us, direct us, or send down a message. Yes, besides the Trinity, we are surrounded by them. They are always watchful and strong protectors. The messages we get leaves us in awe, especially when we know they were responses to our prayers. God sends them to rescue us or help us fight what the enemy throws at us. So that means they are right next to God. Sometimes things happen to us, and it could have been worse, but you know that something interrupted to prevent more hurt. Sometimes someone says something to you that only God knew, and it affirms His message through that person that does not know you that well. God sends angels down, but some are already near us daily. Most importantly, they are the ones we must join in this spiritual battle, as they are constantly fighting for us. So, pick up your weapon (Bible) and fight.

October 1

Squeezed to Be Freed

Answer me when I call to you, O God who declares me innocent. Free me from my troubles. Have mercy on me and hear my prayer. (Psalm 4:1)

We will feel squeezed as God allows us to endure the pressures we need to find freedom. Many of us know those moments when you feel worn out by thinking, striving, waiting, or just battling as more and more piles up. How do people do it without our Great Defender? I cannot imagine their mental state or hearts. Pray for those you know are in that place. The struggles are real for everyone, and the answer to all is Jesus. Being squeezed makes you stronger—yes, vulnerable for a minute, as you are at your capacity, but once you let go and let God, freedom comes, breathing is better, thinking is correct, and anxieties are gone. God must squeeze us to get out what He needs from us to share His truth or take out the hindrances in our way.

October 2

Do You Believe?

"What do you mean, 'If I can'?" Jesus asked. "Anything is possible if a person believes." (Mark 9:23)

To believe means to accept something as true or to feel sure of the truth. We all say we believe until those rough, tough challenges come our way. Some we did not expect, and others we saw slowly approaching and then caved in fear instead of faith. To believe, we need to be strong, trust and know that He will get us through. In storms, this peace will be placed there for a purpose and to help us through, and that stillness is what we need to have to maintain a level of faith that will not cave into emotions that draw us away from Him. We sometimes believe things after seeing them, but God sees us believing in Him first, then His favor comes down. I am not sure about you, but I know I want His favor, blessings, and unconditional love. It gives you comfort like no other. Believe that whatever you think He cannot, He can. In all situations, He wants us to believe. Why would we ever ask if He can? Nothing can stop us from believing but our doubt and fear. He is always for us and with us.

October 3

Blocked

But when I am afraid, I will put my trust in you. (Psalm 56:3)

I use the word "blocked" because when you are on a mission, things come out of nowhere to hinder you, stop you, shake you, or even break you. To get blocked means something got in your way to make it harder or nearly impossible to accomplish your mission. Now, our God was human, but what was impossible for Him? So, with that said, when you want to get in a corner and withdraw when you cannot breathe because the air around you seems to suffocate everything that flows from you, will you stay there? Will you get weaker, more anxious, or frazzled? Will you listen to others who don't even know our God? Or will you grab Jesus's hand and STAND confidently with Him and believe that He comes even in moments you think He is not there. Yes, He knows we get afraid, but He rejoices when He sees us asking Him for help. We overcame those moments that temporarily paralyzed us because our God rescues us when we call.

October 4

Willing to Be Used

So, my dear brothers and sisters, be strong and immovable. Always work enthusiastically for the Lord, for you know that nothing you do for the Lord is ever useless. (1 Corinthians 15:58)

In a time such as this, where the world can consume our thoughts, we can feel that serving God is overwhelming, and when things are not going our way, we think: what is the point in God using us? We keep trying to be that person He calls us to be, but we question: What will come out of this? Who will be blessed by this? What are You doing, God? This sting in us is hurting our hearts, but God does use everything within His timing and purpose. We feel useless because it feels uncomfortable and vulnerable. It is like letting Him do surgery on our hearts to take out all the regrets, hurts, and "whys" and re-stitch us back, so we do not hold on to what inflicts us anymore. But will you allow Him? We know that He is firm and immovable. Why can't we trust Him? He frees us when He does the complete surgery and stitches us with His strong thread.

October 5

What Season Are You In?

For everything there is a season, a time for every activity under heaven. (Ecclesiastes 3:1)

God knew some seasons of our lives were going to trip us up. No one wants to read this, but if the season you are in is a broken season, where everything is falling apart or challenging your faith to the point where you do not see a future, God lets us know there is a purpose that happens to us. It would be best if you took what you went through and learned from it to prevent you from falling into the same trap you know caught you last time. Your heart will deceive if you do not let the Holy Spirit take control of it. Our hearts must be God-centered, not "me" centered. He shows us that not only will we have bad days, but also good days will follow. Not only will we cry, but again, we will laugh (my favorite). It is okay not to be okay, but we must keep going. We are loved and know that hopelessness has no place or time in our lives because God has a good plan. Your focus is to seek and trust Him.

October 6

Replaceable Heart

And I will give them singleness of heart and put a new spirit within them. I will take away their stony, stubborn heart and give them a tender, responsive heart, so they will obey my decrees and regulations. Then they will truly be my people, and I will be their God. (Ezekiel 11:19-20)

God always offered the Israelites a way to change or be obedient to His ways, but they consistently chose to be disobedient. The only way we can follow Jesus is to have a heart that aligns with His practices. Without the Spirit, there is no direction, compassion, unconditional love, or understanding of any expectations. A change of heart must happen because how can a stubborn or selfish one love well? Transformation must occur when following Jesus. We cannot expect to be blessed if all we think about is ourselves or this world that carries so many gods (money, jobs that consume more of our thoughts than God, or anything that takes your time or mind from God). What radiates out of our hearts and our actions will show which God or gods we follow. It is God who gives and takes away from us so that we can live right. Once we make it all about Jesus, everything will fall in place. It is never too late.

Opportunity to be Freed

Therefore, whenever we have the opportunity, we should do good to everyone—especially to those in the family of faith. (Galatians 6:10)

How can we be freed? Well, freedom comes through making things right when God gives us an opportunity to, at the perfect time on a perfect day. Instead of holding it in, could we take this freedom? We do not know if we will get that chance again. Life changes, and we do not want to wish we would have made it right. The verse says to be good to everyone, especially other Christians (those of the family of faith). It may be a challenge but understand this: it is sometimes more challenging to make it right when there is friction with other believers, but if we listen to what God tells us to handle in those moments, we will be okay. God allows us to clear our hearts by freeing us within to be closer to Him and to do His will in our lives wholeheartedly. He wants to enable others to believe that He can change hearts. We cannot do it alone.

October 8

G.P.S

For just as the heavens are higher than the earth, so my ways are higher than your ways and my thoughts higher than your thoughts. (Isaiah 55:9)

Sometimes we start going in a direction but then realize it is a dead-end, so we must turn back and try a different path. This new path can lead to so many possibilities that we would never have imagined. But we only end up at a dead-end when we do not use any guidance from God. God is the best G.P.S. The direction He sends you has no dead end. It is a continuous path that will lead you to His Grace (thank Him for this; we cannot live without it), Promises (thank Him for His words of assurance, strength, and unfailing love covering all of our wrongs, even when we suffer consequences). Salvation (thank You for saving us, fixing us, and allowing our broken hearts to heal so that You can restore them to be stronger than before and heal our minds from the lies the enemy told us). Thank You for showing us to forgive and live and be at peace within ourselves and our journeys.

October 9

Move

I am the LORD, who opened a way through the waters, making a dry path through the sea. (Isaiah 43:16)

Moving is so simple yet so complicated. Move in the direction He is leading, leaving past hurts and people behind. Move to be with those who need you to be beside them. Move without complaining. You get the picture. Sometimes we are just waiting for God's green light. But other times, when He says, "let's go," there is no time to plan or focus on our thoughts or worries. It is just trusting, being obedient, and allowing faith to lead. Sometimes we need a spontaneous movement with boots on the ground, ready to walk, run, jump, or leap. Being prepared to move is being prayed up with pure and understanding hearts. "Lord Jesus, move in each heart that reads this. We do not need the details. You are always with us. Do not leave us and help us to move only when we recognize Your voice (be in His presence). Continue to hold our hands, and may we give You the 110% You deserve. Where You take us will always be the right move. Amen."

October 10

Remember You

For we who worship by the Spirit of God are the ones who are truly circumcised. We rely on what Christ Jesus has done for us. We put no confidence in human effort, though I could have confidence in my own effort if anyone could. Indeed, if others have reason for confidence in their own efforts, I have even more! (Philippians 3:3-4)

It can be so easy to get distracted by a worldly mindset. Yes, it may fulfill you in a moment of fleshly need, but what about your journey on the path with Jesus? Is it worth it? Lord Jesus, remind us who we are today. Could you put it in order? Just one domino of distraction can cause everything and everyone that is connected to your life to fall. No one wants that on them. It is always good to take a step back and evaluate if something in our lives is not in order with God's order. Please fix it. There is no faking it or getting by for now on our journey. Here it goes: others may have hurt us, we may have gotten distracted, we may prioritize being cared for or belonging, or we may have pursued happiness our way instead of God's way. The Way Maker is the only One who will direct our every step, but if you try to manipulate those steps, you can end up on the broad path versus the narrow path. Be the true you in this world even if your flesh is pulling. Pray, seek, and ask, "Is this of You, God, or me?"

October 11

Broken to be Balanced

A time to tear and a time to mend. A time to be quiet and a time to speak. (Ecclesiastes 3:7)

How can we submit to God? It is a process that should not feel like a burden but an honor. The greatest gift we received was salvation. We need to find this balance within, know which way to go, what needs surrendering or who we should step away from our lives. When our character changes, we will become what God requires for His purpose. God must be the center of our lives to find balance; if not, your imbalanced life leads to confusion, lack of direction, or constant struggle. We all are a part of His plan, but He must be the key to your balanced life, the One who levels it all, the One who makes you the "BEST YOU" inside and out. Allow Him to take those burdens weighing you down and start leveling up.

October 12

Believe, Even Though?

But Jesus overheard them and said to Jairus, "Don't be afraid. Just have faith." (Mark 5:36)

Sometimes things come at us so fast that we did not see it coming, and just as quickly, we go down. Then we wonder, what happened? LIFE happened. It is all a part of what we will have to endure. It is not easy: how do you continue when at the moment you cannot see the light that you always look for to keep going, or you cannot hear His voice because other voices around you are so much louder? What do I mean? As fast as you go down is as fast as you need to get back up. Run to clean your eyes so that the light that keeps you going is as bright as the sun within you. We have victory—yes, there will be temporary setbacks—but VICTORY. Block all voices but His; that is all you need to keep going. With bruises and all, we will make it through because He controls all. We must understand and honestly believe it.

October 13

So, So Easy to Get Distracted

Look straight ahead, and fix your eyes on what lies before you. (Proverbs 4:25)

Do not get distracted. The enemy will be on you when he sees you are getting close to a breakthrough. What do you do? Pray that God takes you back to that burning bush moment when He caught your attention. Step back to see what is around you and who is around you (are they lifting you or breaking you down bit by bit?). Pray for God's covering over your mind and heart. Sometimes we get distracted because we are tired of waiting (please wait on God). God's timing is always on time. Keep enduring because He endured more for us. Keep believing you can because Jesus did, and He is our strength, our Rock, and the reason we live and walk today. My prayer for us is that God covers us against distractions. Ask Him to send true friends (no wasting time on friendships that do not pour love or good things in us) and more unconditional love for us to see others through His eyes.

No Answer

But the LORD's plans stand firm forever; his intentions can never be shaken. (Psalm 33:11)

What if there is no answer to what we struggle with daily? Do we get mad at God? Or do we hold on and trust that His plan for us may sometimes come with or without answers. As deep struggles, challenges, and hardships increase, Jesus will go deeper to save us from all of it. I know that is part of my testimony, and I know I am not alone in this. I hear "Amen" already. The verse says that God's plans stand firm forever, so that means it will not waver. It will reach its aim or goal. Nothing can stop it, but bruising will occur, people will be added or removed from our lives, and we will mature in the process and understand in the end. "Lord Jesus, the only place we want to be in is the place of YOUR will, no one else's. Amen."

Making it Right

Now let your unfailing love comfort me, just as you promised me, your servant. (Psalm 119:76)

His unfailing love is our comfort—so true. God's love is the only true love that does not hold grudges against us when we fail Him. He knows the battles with us, others, and the world that we face. So, yes, it is a comfort to have this love that says we are enough, which He proved on the cross and that says we have no reason to hold onto things from our past as all of it was forgiven. But our flesh does deceive us when we leave an open area for the enemy to enter and attack insecurities; this can cause us to doubt that He loves us with this love. Here it goes: if He forgives us, we must forgive as well—with genuine hearts, not one grudge can remain. Put it in prayer for your heart to be freed from burdens so that you will grow in your faith. You are worthy, forgiven, loved, and strong. Do not give up because He will not.

Never Abandoned

The LORD will work out his plans for my life—for your faithful love, O LORD, endures forever. Don't abandon me, for you made me. (Psalm 138:8)

God assures us that He is not leaving. He has a plan; know this and accept this. We cannot change what is already in motion. If God is leading, then follow. The last line says, "don't abandon me" and "you made me." Some of us know that this hits deep—being abandoned by a parent, in a marriage, or a friendship hurts, especially when you don't see it coming. But God does not at any point leave you unless you detach from Him by way of your sin, which He cannot accept unless we repent. He is Holy. He does not go because the One who created us would have no reason to abandon when the creation (us) has a purpose, has His love placed inside to spread, and has an assignment to complete. I saw the word "insurmountable" (too great to overcome) and thought of this journey. Nothing is too great for God's children to overcome.

Invested

You must each decide in your heart how much to give. And don't give reluctantly or in response to pressure. "For God loves a person who gives cheerfully." (2 Corinthians 9:7)

We invest (put or give our time into some-thing or someone), but what are we reaping? Are we happy? Content? Is what is expected from us enough? Doing the right thing because that is who we are? Are we people pleasers or God-seekers? We will find that perfect peace from making an impact with our giving hearts that help others, knowing God will always provide a personal decision. Are we invested in God's Kingdom or not? Will you give Him your all (talent, time, money, and God-given gifts)? To benefit from what we put into following God, we must wholeheartedly want to do it. When you hear, "you will reap the benefits," know that is true. Just ask those God-seekers who never give up, who always follow God in all seasons, who keep going no matter what, or who try to discourage them. Blessed are they because He sees their giving and cheerful hearts.

What Are You Working For?

Work willingly at whatever you do, as though you were working for the Lord rather than for people.
(Colossians 3:23)

The Bible says to work as if you were working for the Lord. Let us think about this: there is so much pressure, anxiety, fear, and doubt every day. We wonder if we will meet expectations and have so many questions. What else do you carry that has your mind, heart, and body working overtime on always? What is work? It is an activity involving physical or mental effort to achieve a purpose or result. Okay, here it goes: are we working toward Jesus, or are we wasting time? Yes, we work and get paid. But now apply it to your journey. Are we getting up early to hear Him? Are we putting in overtime during those hard seasons? Are we late because we were entertaining things not of God? Work toward Him, and you will never lose. Do not waste more time. You will see the results of the work put in. Yes, it can wear you out, but it is better to be tired of God than to be drained by the world. His work package includes a feeling of peace and a clear mind.

Anybody Need Wisdom?

But when you ask him, be sure that your faith is in God alone. Do not waver, for a person with divided loyalty is as unsettled as a wave of the sea that is blown and tossed by the wind. (James 1:6)

To receive, we must not be in divided mindsets. You cannot ask God for something and not have faith that He can provide it. Nor can you ask Him for something as you follow the beliefs or ways of this world. If you are tired of the same results, then go back and start over, but put your faith in God alone. No more accepting what the world says about things. No more "I don't know how to pray." Praying is only talking to God with an honest heart. No more lies because He knows you. No more tug-of-war within your heart between God's or enemy's way (world); the pressure is no longer a burden. It is straightforward: God wins every battle. Yes, it is easier said than done. All we have is His promises, truth, and direction. We know that He chose us during the worst times of our lives, and He changed us so that we do not go back but rather move forward and share who He is with others. Ask Him what you need and give Him your heart. The world will never provide you what God alone gives. It may look good, but it will never come close to God. Do not settle for anything unless God gives it. If no one has ever said it to you, I will: YOU are worth so much more.

If This Was Your Last Day

Don't brag about tomorrow, since you do not know what the day will bring. (Proverbs 27:1)

Sometimes as you think about your last day, your emotions get the best of you. We want to do so much, but we do not make intentional time for those things. Sometimes we neglect to share our thoughts and true feelings with family and friends. So, what does this mean? Do not live a life of regret, not doing something you could have done. Enjoy yourself as much as you can. Be YOU without worrying if you meet anyone else's standards. Genuine people will accept you the way you are. Share the story of Jesus; spread the Word, try new things, and choose to be different. Do not follow the world; follow the One who rules the world. I say I love you all the time to those who have touched my heart because I never want anyone ever to wonder what they meant to me. Say it to someone today if you have not. Forgive others; it is only for your freedom and release. Do all this so that the blessings can pour down, as tomorrow will not be a promise to anyone.

Time for Your Inner Work

That is why we never give up. Though our bodies are dying, our spirits are being renewed every day. (2 Corinthians 4:16)

Every day is a new day to work on letting God do what He alone can do in our lives. But to accomplish what needs to be changed or adjusted in our lives, He needs our undivided attention. Yes, that is what I mean. How can He do what He does best if we do not take the time to schedule Him in our lives? How else can we hear Him or feel Him? It is not only making time for Him to listen to our cries, but it is also making time to refresh daily, reset, be renewed, and be encouraged by Him. His promises are real, but He needs that stillness from us. I pray for a moment of serenity for all of us, just an uninterrupted moment to be with Him. Forgive us for sometimes not prioritizing YOU, our WAYMAKER.

October 22

Reflections of You

The LORD has punished me severely, but he did not let me die. (Psalm 118:18)

This one may hit home for some of us, but I love to go here because it reminds us of God's grace and faithfulness during challenges. Yes, it may be sad, but look at where you are now. It is not perfect, but still, press on. You will find new friends, new experiences, and new meaning in your life that you never thought of before. I pray for God to continue showing the truth of who you are. What do you still hold on to when He says, "Let go?" Is there anything that keeps you stagnant on this journey? Are you tired of running around in circles, still at the same place in your heart and mind? Be you, but let God mold you, change you, and stir you up, even if He breaks you a little. Let Him show you through the Bible. Hear Him say, "I have so much for you, but I need you to trust Me, not block Me when I correct you." Sometimes we will need help from others. The Spirit will guide you to that person. Just ask for prayer.

October 23

Only for Him

All who are mine belong to you, and you have given them to me, so they bring me glory. (John 17:10)

Are we doing this daily? Give Him the glory always, in all situations in the good, bad, ugliest, or most challenging moments. This verse reminds us that He chose us, and we belong to Jesus—let us stay in this thinking. It is all genuine, authentic, accurate, honest, and unconditional love; this has to motivate each one of us as we walk in authority: He has given us to do, be, show and apply all our faith that will glorify Him. If we are not showing His character daily to others or giving Him glory—who are we representing—ourselves, others, or the world? What stops us from glorifying Him, the cliché of our "flesh," is getting old, or is it an excuse not to do? I pray everyone has an opportunity to experience something that will give God the glory He deserves and that we get to be witnesses of it; it is an honor and privilege to stand with Him in those moments.

October 24

Mend the World or Ourselves?

Put on your new nature, and be renewed as you learn to know your Creator and become like him. (Colossians 3:10)

We walk this journey and pray that God would mend what needs to be fixed so that nothing withholds the blessings He has for us. Let us look at ourselves before we try to restore the world and renew every area of our lives, and may we wait patiently throughout the process. Although we live in this world, we are not a part of it. So, this daily repair of self is needed. Please take out the bad and replace it with goodness. It is like a chain of beads of different colors (each unique). We each hold a separate piece. For this chain to be created or finished, everyone must do their part to connect.

When Will You Truly Say Enough?

Then he went on alone into the wilderness, traveling all day. He sat down under a solitary broom tree and prayed that he might die. "I have had enough, LORD," he said. "Take my life, for I am no better than my ancestors who have already died." (1 Kings 19:4)

If we do not sincerely say we have reached our limit, how can God help? The keywords in this verse are alone, solitary, enough, and take my life. Put it in a spiritual perspective: to hear God, we need to be alone in solitude and prayer to let Him know that we have had enough and then surrender our life to Him. We need spiritual food (His words and promises) to sustain us for this Christian journey. Our trials can be overwhelming, so eat as much as you can so that you have the strength to make it through. God gives rest if we ask, so if anyone is in a season of overload, at the edge of self, or needs to breathe, I pray this helps you. Tell God, "I need You to reset my mind, heart, and thoughts." Always acknowledge and know that God is in control; we do not have to understand; we must follow and be obedient.

October 26

No Dwelling on Concerns

Don't worry about anything; instead, pray about everything. Tell God what you need, and thank him for all he has done. (Philippians 4:6)

How do we avoid worry when everything around us is trying to pull us down? Sometimes we do not get a chance to breathe and want everything to stop for just a moment. At that moment, we need to be under His wings for safety, rejuvenation, peace of mind, love, hope, restoration, renewed perspective, or to breathe. God says not to worry: because everything I just said and more is what He offers us if we give it to Him. He takes care of it. The hurt will still sting, but we can tolerate it and endure it because of His protection over our hearts and minds. Jesus's peace is what we need. Once you understand that, nothing will surprise you or continue to pull you down. We must remember always to thank Him when the waves of life hit hard and when the waves are calm. You will be taken to the next level in your spiritual journey if you keep persevering. Who does not want that?

Worthy Qualities

So we keep on praying for you, asking our God to enable you to live a life worthy of his call. May he give you the power to accomplish all the good things your faith prompts you to do. (2 Thessalonians 1:11)

With everything going on in this world, we can lose some of that faith poured into us. But the opposite is happening as well. Some of us have increased our confidence because we know believing in God is not a part-time job. We cannot let go of Him when the tough times come. Instead, we run as fast as we can. We learn more, hold on tighter, and dig deeper into His words and promises. Emotions will shake us. Even when our loved ones are scared, our faith needs to be more evident in these times. God gives us the authority to pray and be who He called us to be. We are worthy in Jesus, so live like it. We have the power to do good, so stop wasting any time on destructive behaviors that do not benefit God. If we focus on making our faith stronger, we will help others see God the way we do. Our calling is to spread Jesus and do good always, even during threatening situations.

Is It That God Is Too Good to Be True?

The LORD is good and does what is right; he shows the proper path to those who go astray. (Psalm 25:8)

He offers so much during our struggles. Do you see it? How can God be in control of what we go through? Our pain? Even when we do not let go of things or people that He warned us to let go of, our willful act wanted its way? Even when we refuse to submit? In the end, He took it away anyway. But understand this: He is in control of all things whether we know it or not. He will flip a bad situation into a good one. The free will that we use is not His fault, especially when things turn out bad. Some try to justify it because they do not want to accept responsibility for their actions. We must take it; God knows and still loves us. Repent and follow Him. Yes, do, be, and show that you know what is right. Some will say you are too nice. Yeah, words can hurt, but if they do not understand who you are and why you strive for the goodness that God has given you, do not take offense to it. Let it go and love more.

October 29

The Most of Us

Make the most of every opportunity in these evil days. Don't act thoughtlessly, but understand what the Lord wants you to do. (Ephesians 5:16-17)

We get the opportunity to show Jesus's character to others through text, social media, or in person. It is about taking the chance and doing the most with it to the greatest extent. Put all of you in whatever God tells you to do or who He shows you to share yourself with then you will see your part in His plan. We are not always honest with everyone; that is the truth. Be thoughtful in action, not careless. No wasting time—Jesus did not waste time. Every moment is a teachable moment if we are attentive and focused on what He wants us to do. Be considerate of others. We all have a story. Some struggles may be worse, but we all overcame them when we fully surrendered. Some may still be trying to overcome, but it is a process. God found us and connected us for a reason. "Thank you, Jesus, for everyone you have sent our way to help us or for us to help them. Amen."

No Other Voice Should Direct

Your own ears will hear him. Right behind you a voice will say, "This is the way you should go," whether to the right or to the left. (Isaiah 30:21)

How many times has God directed you and said, "go there" or "go talk to this person," and you end up being an answered prayer for them? Sometimes it is loud and clear, and other times we must have too much ear wax buildup (can I be honest) that we do not hear Him. Maybe we do hear, but it is very distant, or, honestly, we ignore Him (remember free will) and go the opposite direction. Yes, you got it: we end up nowhere—sometimes in a worse situation, sometimes the same problem in a different season. Isn't it tiring and exhausting to make decisions without Jesus? What if He is the first to know the dilemma that troubles your heart? Do you trust Him? Saying I believe it is not just singing a song, raising your hand, or dancing. Our hearts must be so excited from believing, trusting, and knowing that where He directs will be right.

Knowing His Name

And this is the way to have eternal life—to know you, the only true God, and Jesus Christ, the one you sent to earth. (John 17:3)

To know His name is to see the power that comes with it. Fear has no place if we are grounded in our relationship with Jesus. Especially in these times that we are in, we believe the blood of Jesus covers us or keeps us from going further down the wide path resulting in getting more lost, confused, or anxious. Knowing and accepting His name is knowing how strong we are. It believes we can survive the hardest hits in life that we do not want to face but know we must. During these times, God is speaking. Being in isolation is not always a bad thing. For those who love to be in His presence, it is a time to find answers for who they are, discern the next steps for what God wants them to do, or just rest. God always finds a way to get our attention for our overall well-being. There is no stronger name than Jesus.

November 1

Into Your Hands

Give all your worries and cares to God, for he cares about you. (1 Peter 5:7)

I love this. God says to cast all our cares on Him—not some cares, all. I know we are stubborn; sometimes we struggle with letting go, and He knows that, but try to give one thing at a time. I pray for the peace of mind and that you hear Him loud and clear. I pray that you dare to admit you have limitations and know that our God does not. His grace is what we want. I am not saying to let go smoothly. That is the most challenging part, but our God is faithful, bigger than our struggles, and never gets tired of hearing our prayers.

Let It Go

If you cling to your life, you will lose it, and if you let your life go, you will save it. (Luke 17:33)

Yes, as we cling to our lives, we try to control every aspect of it, who will be in or out of our hearts, jobs we strive to get that stress us out, continually feeding our souls with materialism and living in grey areas (one foot in and one foot out) in our faith. And wonder why we are not content with everything we control. The Bible says we save ourselves by letting go of holding onto our lives. Yes, let go means let God. Our flesh always fights what is spiritually true. If anyone is clinging to their life, I know you must be tired. No life without Jesus will save or strengthen you because He is peace, love, and that drive to hope. Give your life to Him and His ways, and you will find yourself 110% guaranteed.

November 3

One Source Provides

There are different kinds of spiritual gifts, but the same Spirit is the source of them all. (1 Corinthians 12:4)

Seek and pray to God to help you in knowing your spiritual gifts if you do not already. You may have the advantage of wisdom, discernment, or leading others to God. Yes, in your gift, you will feel comfortable, confident, and motivated. How do we know? Because God did not give it to us for us to struggle in trying to figure it out. Maybe we are too distracted to see it clearly or not committed to Him completely, so we cannot sense His presence or hear Him. He gives us time to think about applying it, but do not waste your character or personality uniqueness. Some of us attract people right away, and some of us do not. There is a reason for it. We are all needed, wanted, and have a purpose. As the verse states, God is the source of all gifts we receive. The enemy makes us feel like we have no meaning because he knows that he loses control over us once we find our advantage. Remember who gets all the glory when our gifts are used for His purpose to help others.

Human

So the Word became human and made his home among us. He was full of unfailing love and faithfulness. And we have seen his glory, the glory of the Father's one and only Son. (John 1:14)

Yes, the Word (Jesus) became like us so that we can become like Him. It is not an acting role or faking love, but it genuinely cares for others with the heart of Jesus, even if you get rejected. Even if others just do not get it, God works in them to see it. They may take longer as they fight the struggle of putting all that sadness, bitterness, or unforgiveness at His feet. The verse states that Jesus was full of love and faithfulness, so we must be for others whether they love us back or not. We must honor what He expects from us. You do not know who will grab on, but God always goes before us and opens the hearts of others to receive our unconditional love. Go where He sends you, even if you feel uncomfortable. We work for God's approval, not people. Jesus will need your presence to give hope to others during their pain. Be selfless, not selfish. Our flesh should be saving, not sinning.

S.H.U.T. D.O.W.N.

For God speaks again and again, though people do not recognize it. (Job 33:14)

What do you think leads to God shutting something down? Can it be that God is now speaking louder, as He was not listened to before? Can it be that enough is enough? Can it be that He wonders why His creation is not genuinely caring for the things or people He wants us to care for in this world? Yeah, everything must stop for a reason. God wants us to stop so that we may experience (S)olitude—a self-examination of where we are, an increase in (H)umility and (U)nity, and our (T)rust in God's will rise as we (D)are to believe again. (O)bedience is necessary, (W)orship Him in crisis, and (N)ever give up on Him. We are unique, forgiven, and will rise again if we have fallen. Put God above all, and our lives will change if we do not waver. God will prove His point.

Find Him, Live Right and Receive

Seek the Kingdom of God above all else, and live righteously, and he will give you everything you need. (Matthew 6:33)

Seeking (making attempts to find some-thing) is what we spend our lives doing—whether to find a good-paying job, the right person, the right path, or answers to confusing situations. Sometimes we are lucky and discover what we seek, and the answer is love and peace of mind. And sometimes, we do not find it because Jesus is not in it. Certain things just will not come until we invite Him into our hearts. We seek to use our strength, knowledge, or abilities, and all we do is get worn out. Living right is not easy, as the world's standards and people can confuse us, but it will ease the burden if we remember we are not of this world. If we are grounded in our faith, we are stronger and handle these struggles better because He goes before us. Put God first above everyone and every-thing, and He will bless you with all of your essentials. Do not ever let anyone make you feel that you lose when you walk with Jesus. He is all we need to LIVE. With Him, you will always be a winner.

November 7

Daily Necessity

I have not departed from his commands, but have treasured his words more than daily food. (Job 23:12)

Job, a man who feared God, was tested. As he was experiencing those difficult moments, he always held on to God's words. It was more important to him than food. In the same way, food is necessary for us to live, so should God's word be. What would life be if we did not have His words to hold us up, hold us together, direct our path, direct our decisions, or even give us a wake-up call when we mess up and hurt others without thinking? Like food nourishes the body, His words are necessary for our minds and gives us strength to continue. Only they are more intense, more powerful, and bring better results. God's words are always available without restriction, and we have control over how much we listen to them. Value what you know and keep adding to it to become more assertive in your journey. Food for thought: the best and only treasure we can ever attain is God.

Life Without Jesus

What if the LORD had not been on our side when people attacked us? (Psalm 124:2)

How often have we been in situations that got out of control, but then we prayed, and it was resolved by following God's instructions? What if we did not have Him as an option? What if we did not have those instructions? What if we did not have any connection to Him? Or, to be honest, are some of us there now? I would think it feels burdensome and heavy. There is no need to be in that place because Jesus always welcomes us back if we have strayed—no questions asked (He already knows). Accept the discipline if He must give it because, in reality, if we do wrong in the sight of God, we will have to suffer the consequences, which is fair. Once we are right with Him, there is no going back, just forward in peace, unconditional love, and contentment. Do right as best as you can, endure through hard times, and know that He will take control when we trust and believe. We need Him on our side.

Highly Qualified

It is not that we think we are qualified to do anything on our own. Our qualification comes from God. (2 Corinthians 3:5)

This statement is for all who feel they do not have what it takes to do God's will. Only One gives these qualifications (a quality that makes someone suitable for a job) to accomplish His purpose. Leading others to Christ is not hard if you are willing to share your testimony when the Spirit leads you to. What makes us qualified is telling the truth of what we went through, what we felt, what we endured, or what broke us to cause us to seek Jesus. You are qualified to tell the impact of His presence on your life to others. Pray for God to bring those who are searching. Now is the time to help the curious or help those who are tired of searching in the wrong places. To be qualified means that we will walk with God's unconditional love, direction, correction at times, a trusting heart when things do not make sense, unwavering faith during the struggle, and the strength to walk in boldness where He sends us.

Suffering Like Jesus

For God called you to do good, even if it means suffering, just as Christ suffered for you. He is your example, and you must follow in his steps. (1 Peter 2:21)

It cannot be a surprise that we will suffer if we want to follow God. Especially if you do the things God calls you to do. You will feel that pulling of your heart to go the way He is leading you. Your first reaction may be, "Am I qualified to do your will, God?" Anyone who knows that intimacy with God knows He speaks, He assures, calms the fears, and He refocuses us to remember why we walk this earth (for His purpose). The verse says that God calls us to do good even if we suffer. No one wants to suffer any pain, any sadness, any betrayal, or any brokenness, but Jesus did and remained sinless. He teaches us that we need to stay focused on Him and His instructions, not to let things or people distract us. He teaches us to pour more and more love out to those searching and continue to be consistent in studying His words of truth. When you experience struggles and suffering, hold on tighter to Him.

November 11

The House

I was glad when they said to me, "Let us go to the house of the LORD." (Psalm 122:1)

We all find comfort in our homes, especially in this pandemic where we had no choice but to stay home, and even now, we still must be careful. But we also lost the physical place of meeting God with other believers. The following happens: fellowship, laughter, comfort, crying, cafe conversations, hearing spoken words that God gives our Pastors, and seeing healing through prayers. The church can be intimidating because once we step in and come with open hearts, He will come knocking or heal our brokenness. Some step in because they know God must have more for them, and it is a place of security of who they belong to in this world. Not being in the house of the Lord should not discourage us; it should encourage us that we get more time to seek Him by ourselves so He can equip us for what is coming. God's house reminds us to stay grounded, keep going and know who we are: chosen by Jesus.

November 12

Need Someone

Along the way, they came across a man named Simon, who was from Cyrene, and the soldiers forced him to carry Jesus' cross. (Matthew 27:32)

Even Jesus needed someone to help Him carry the cross. Do we believe that? He doesn't need anyone, but maybe He wanted us to visualize what it is to carry our crosses and for a moment for Simon to feel what it is to take someone else's burden. But even with that, let us never forget that Jesus was before him and with him. To take our crosses each day faithfully is so hard when the weight is heavy. May we ask for help when it is needed. To be God's beloved, we will sometimes be taken back to parts of our story (people, sadness, or our testimonies) that will keep us real, honest, and vulnerable and lead us to the truth of who we are. It is evident how He healed us. Those parts of ourselves, even if spoken with tears, will help with our cross. It does not mean we do not have faith or are not grateful to God; it just means this journey is difficult. He never said it would be easy, but He did say He would never leave us, and I know He always goes before us.

You Are All I Got

I know the LORD is always with me. I will not be shaken, for he is right beside me. (Psalm 16:8)

Visualize a ladder: each step you are going up, losing layers of yourself, such as your struggle with the world versus Jesus. Continue to climb up, seeking Jesus, and as you keep going up, you will wrestle with your identity. Keep climbing, and surrender will happen, but sometimes only partially, as fear takes hold of you. Giving everything will cause a massive shift, and as we surrender, it can be challenging for us to do for our spiritual well-being. But the journey is NOT partial. So, think of other steps you will encounter until you get to the top, where you will find peace, freedom, and hope; this is our aim. To succeed is to know who your priority is and at what cost. Is Jesus worth climbing up this ladder? Aren't you worth the climb? Either way, you make that choice. It will require work, you will get hurt, and there is a cost. Jesus knows you are worth it and strong enough to climb, even if you slip sometimes. Breathe, then keep going up. No coming down back to what does not matter anymore.

Peace is a Weapon

For shoes, put on the peace that comes from the Good News so that you will be fully prepared. (Ephesians 6:15)

As long as you plant your feet in God's promises, the enemy might be able to shake you a little bit (if you are not ready), but he will never break you if you walk with your shoes secured in God's peace. Stand firm, be in your ready position always, and as you move with this peace, share the gospel (Good News) that gives the hopeless a peace they have never had before; this backfires on the enemy. Someone saved is one less person off the enemy's list that will no longer be in bondage. Also, as he throws doubt, your peace shoes should be grounded & standing on God's word so that you can be in a position with your arrows of scriptures you have memorized to defend yourselves.

OUTSTRETCHED FAITH / 337

Truth—Protects Us from the Enemy

But we belong to God, and those who know God listen to us. If they do not belong to God, they do not listen to us. That is how we know if someone has the Spirit of truth or spirit of deception. (1 John 4:6)

God's truth is the only truth we should be concerned with, but the problem is the enemy is good at playing with our minds and turning truth into confusion. So, we need to be ready to protect ourselves when lies creep upon us. Look in your Bible to see what God's truth reveals. There is no arrow the enemy can shoot at us that we cannot block with scriptures' facts. The truth is our God is all-knowing, unchangeable, unstoppable, unmovable, unbreakable, faithful, loving, gracious, forgiving, and is in control of all things. We need to cling to that. I pray that you may see or hear the truth of God, whether a text, a conversation, or a tangible item that reminds you of where you once were and the truth that saved YOU.

November 16

Spiritual Point of View

So we have stopped evaluating others from a human point of view. At one time we thought of Christ merely from a human point of view. How differently we know him now! This means that anyone who belongs to Christ has become a new person. The old life is gone; a new life has begun! (2 Corinthians 5:16-17)

We all have a voice and perspectives on how to understand people or things that happen to us; yes, we were made unique by God and with a DNA with characteristics that God will tweak when He chooses us to do His will. Our thoughts followed a human perspective before saved, but now we see our ideas, behaviors, and attitudes on things or people changed. He shows us a perspective that follows His principles, compassion for others' pain, and His heart to lead them to Him. If we follow our spiritual perspective as Jesus did, we will handle life better, but it does not mean life will be easy. We begin to see things as a test of faith, character, or another thing added to mature in our walk versus hating the world for everything that happens to us, blaming others for our hurts and our walk (everyone is responsible for their own). What point of view will you follow?

Wise Decision

"But blessed are those who trust in the LORD and have made the LORD their hope and confidence. (Jeremiah 17:7)

The keywords in this verse are "have made." Decide to choose God—our hope, trust, and confidence–, and we will be blessed. Life challenges or old wounds of the heart not dealt with will someday bring us to this crossroad. To choose God is to let go of self (selfish ways, pride, negative thinking, judgmental thinking, or anything that does not show compassion for others). We must genuinely believe that He is for us and stop trying to do it all alone, as you will see that we do not get far without Him. Trusting in Him is not always easy, as there are expectations, but He is the pilot of our lives and knows our destination. Talk it out with God; give it to Him to take care of and trust Him. God shows us the truth about ourselves, even if it hurts. Love yourselves, trust Him with everything within you, and be blessed, and you will find that confidence you are seeking. No one else can provide what will make you complete.

Small

Do not despise these small beginnings, for the LORD rejoices to see the work begin, to see the plumb line in Zerubbabel's hand." (The seven lamps represent the eyes of the LORD that search all around the world.) (Zechariah 4:10)

Always thank God for the small moments that He gave us of love and peace. May we remember that He is a seed within us that we need to water by reading the Bible, worshiping, praising, and praying. Our connection with Him is not to help us do small things but is to empower us to do tremendous and more significant things in our lives for Him. We must be obedient and know that whatever little blessing He gives us will have a significant meaning behind it. Small steps today will provide us a bigger and better future because His Spirit will not leave us—especially when we struggle in life. I pray that God removes anyone we encounter or lies from the enemy that tells us this small situation does not matter to God. May we understand that everything about us matters to Him, and may we be witnesses to each time a life is changed.

November 19

Grace

For the law was given through Moses, but God's unfailing love and faithfulness came through Jesus Christ. (John 1:17)

What would we do without this grace that Jesus gives us every day? It is so needed, and we do not deserve it. Grace means favor or kindness expressed to the undeserving. Yes, this means being friendly to the ones who challenge us. Did I hit a nerve? Sometimes God is trying to show us how to look deep within and see what He sees: someone as broken as we are and someone who may need a little patience or help to let down their walls to get back on track. You may be surprised by what you learn. Everyone has a story, broken in different ways, and desires for someone to care without judgment. The cross shows His grace for us and is an example for us to follow as we need to give it to others.

Deserted by All

On the way, Jesus told them, "All of you will desert me. For the Scriptures say, 'God will strike the Shepherd, and the sheep will be scattered.' (Mark 14:27)

This verse made me think about what my Pastor once said regarding the last supper about how the disciples must have felt after Jesus said He was going to be betrayed by one of them. It states, *"Greatly distressed, each one asked in turn, "Am I the one?"* (Mark 14:19). I'm sure they probably wondered who would do it. They probably questioned how He knew that He was about to be betrayed or thought it would not be them. But they may not have all betrayed Him at the same severity, but they all did leave Him. Was it fear? Confusion? Safety? Yeah, how many times have we deserted Him for things or people that do not even come close to what He offers us? But even knowing what was going to happen, He still loved them. Yes, He still loves us even when we turn away from Him. The enemy says Jesus will not take us back or forgive us for our sins, but we know He will if we genuinely repent and change our ways to His ways.

Be Anxious

You won't spend the rest of your lives chasing your own desires, but you will be anxious to do the will of God. (1 Peter 4:2)

Now I know that your mind will jump to the anxious mode when you read the title, but I am not saying what you may be thinking. All that walk in the discipline of seeking God can always vouch for this. We all know what it feels like to have anxieties. Yes, this can be a feeling, but it can also be a desire to do something. If you know me, I always have that desire to jump in to help or do; that is just who I am. I know many of you carry that same mindset, and we go into an anxious mode when we cannot be there physically to help for whatever reason. But as you read in this verse, you will find that this mindset happens because as you seek and deeply commit yourself to God, His will takes over your desires. So, when He says go, we go. We get anxious because He chooses us. We may not understand where He is sending us and why, but it does not matter because we trust Him. Let us not forget it is all for His will.

November 22

Tragedy to Triumph

Then Jesus uttered another loud cry and breathed his last. (Mark 15:37)

What words can you say to Jesus other than "thank you" and "forgive us?" Some of those stripes on His body have our names on them. Not to make us feel bad, but He died for each of us. No other being could be as strong as our King, who endured all. He pushed through and focused on the mission as He carried the cross. It was a long walk to take, as people were cruel to Him, but He forgives. What is on your cross that keeps knocking you down? Are you staying down? Are you getting back up and finally following Jesus? Are you waiting for someone to pick it up for you, or do you need help for just a moment? The most honest soul who carries us each day suffered on that cross for our wrongdoings and still gives us free will. Yeah, we need to feel it that deep. Sadly, it had to happen for us to be right with God.

I AM

Jesus said, "I AM. And you will see the Son of Man seated in the place of power at God's right hand and coming on the clouds of heaven." (Mark 14:62)

What else do we need to know other than these words are of God? Jesus was betrayed, arrested, beaten, mistreated, and humiliated. We know we cannot see it coming with human eyes, but divinely He saw it all. God created love, not anger, bitterness, unforgiveness, or hatred. There is no peace in any of that. We think we can handle it, but it destroys everything that God has for us. Picture this: Jesus is in front of you saying, "I AM all that you need. I AM your father. I AM who you hold on to when you feel you cannot. I AM love. I AM truth always—no lies with Me. I AM your only hope. I AM the only One who can show you the Way. I AM the one who can bring out your faith and use it for good (focus only on what I say). I AM the one who gave you your life and knew the plans for you. I AM the one who forgives you and shows you that to be with Me, you must have a forgiving heart." Jesus believed that we were worth it, but do we think He is worth it?

Wake Up Call

The LORD opens the eyes of the blind. The LORD lifts up those who are weighed down. The LORD loves the godly. (Psalm 146:8)

What does it take for someone to open their eyes and see God? Or to stop playing the hide-and-seek game with Him? He is the One who controls all the fun in our lives, but somehow, we use free will and do not choose Him until something shakes us. It also states that God opens our eyes, He lifts us, and He loves us. God has healed physical blindness and corrects our spiritual blindness if we ask Him for help. We all need it as we try to get through each day with this new norm. We find comfort in knowing that God loves all who follow Him during the most challenging days when we cannot comfort each other. He knows and allows us to give Him all that tries to keep us discouraged. How can we not see beyond the world and realize that only He offers what we need to survive?

Final Control

And I know that whatever God does is final. Nothing can be added to it or taken from it. God's purpose is that people should fear him. (Ecclesiastes 3:14)

We may want to ask God so many things because we are questioning that shift in our lives, but sometimes we are scared to hear the answer. God should be our best friend, so be REAL with Him. We should fear Him; this will keep us from doing further damage to ourselves. Fearing God shows respect to Him by not doing things that disrespect His character (remember, His journey to the cross should put us back on track). The verse says what He does is final, and nothing can be added or taken from it. During certain seasons in our lives, we have had final moments that were hard. He is always in those moments, but we must endure them and walk away learning something from them. When He reveals your purpose, it is what He says it is. We may not know what to expect, but we know that it will change our inner being. We can pray others will understand, but obedience to Him is what comes first. No one can change what God starts in our season.

November 26

Walking Away from Jesus

And my righteous ones will live by faith. But I will take no pleasure in anyone who turns away."
(Hebrews 10:38)

Some may walk away thinking that Jesus can be on hold. They have their reasons, but the saddest thing to witness is someone walking away and missing out on what He had for them. When we turn away from Him, we step away from His covering. He watches our self-destruction, and it is not pleasing at all to Him; this brings no peace, contentment, guidance, or clarity. The purpose of the cross was to end the pain, not cause more pain for ourselves and Him. Or was it all for nothing? Keep walking in your faith daily, but know you must pass the test that shows your faith level stands. Is your religion going to rise or break? Will you continue to follow or turn away when the cost is higher? Do you want a soul saved or shattered? The narrow path that leads to Jesus is to go forward, not backward. Even though the pillars of life will fall on us, our seed of faith will give us the strength to push them off of our path as we keep moving forward.

The Word is a
Chain Reaction

So take a new grip with your tired hands and strengthen your weak knees. Mark out a straight path for your feet so that those who are weak and lame will not fall but become strong. (Hebrews 12:12-13)

Just like a domino effect, as one starts falling, it knocks down the next one, then the next. In our journey, when one person starts sharing Jesus, it deposits into the next person, then continues creating a solid chain that makes the weak stronger. Here are the keywords: new grip, strengthen, straight path, and strong. Let us apply this right now: struggles can cause many to fear, or they can cause us to tighten our grip on Jesus. Do not let go; this is where we hold on tighter to His words and the hem of His garment. The only way we can strengthen our minds, and physical self is by getting closer to Jesus. In His presence, we help set that straight and narrow path for others who do not know which way to go. As they follow, they do not get weaker but stronger. "We are in this together" is what we hear all the time, so help someone you know that is struggling right now, especially spiritually, as some believers are losing hope.

350 \ CARMEN M. RODRIGUEZ

Highly Favored

But whatever I am now, it is all because God poured out his special favor on me—and not without results. For I have worked harder than any of the other apostles; yet it was not I but God who was working through me by his grace. (1 Corinthians 15:10)

It is important to remember that once you become a Christian, you can sometimes hold on to your old self that God has forgiven. The only thing that matters is who you are now and how you will allow God to take you to that next level. You will see results when He pours into you and works through you. What does He pour into us? He has a good character, a compassionate heart, unconditional love, and understanding of people. So, yes, He is a Father who teaches us to make sure no one will be left behind. He will find a way to save each soul. He already works through us by empowering us to share. When others believe, it is evident that it is working, so keep doing it. Do not let fear paralyze your determination to share Him. There are lost souls waiting for someone to share this Jesus, who loves so much and frees us from any bondage of the heart and mind. He chose you to do this for Him.

November 29

Give Him All

"I tell you the truth," Jesus said, "this poor widow has given more than all the rest of them. For they have given a tiny part of their surplus, but she, poor as she is, has given everything she has." (Luke 21:3-4)

We are to create new habits as we lean on Jesus. Will we give Him everything within us and all that we have, trusting that He will continue to provide for us? As you read in this verse, you will find that whatever you give to God, He sees and honors, especially when it comes from a humble, genuine, and honest heart. Giving to God, we never lose and only gain more. What do we achieve? His favor, trust, being seen, loved, understood, provided for, learning to be content and appreciate the little we have when we cannot have a surplus. The poor widow gave what she had. Was it because of her faith that she says, "I don't have much, but here it is God; I trust You and thank You for taking care of me?" Maybe she knew that having God is being rich spiritually; what more can she ask from Him? Will you give Him everything, even if it will cost you everything, including letting go of others or things?

Firewood Needed

This is why I remind you to fan into flames the spiritual gift God gave you when I laid my hands on you. For God has not given us a spirit of fear and timidity, but of power, love, and self-discipline. (2 Timothy 1:6-7)

When you want to keep the flames going, you must fuel them to increase their strength. Similarly, our spiritual gifts need strengthening in the fire, or the purpose will be harder to accomplish. Paul is encouraging Timothy of his spiritual gifts. We need to activate it using God's power, love, and discipline. Anyone who knows their gift will agree. We will always need firewood to put in our spiritual flames: 1) Know who you are without wavering. 2) Love unconditionally, whether they deserve it or not. 3) Practice self-discipline in all areas of your life; pour into Him, and He will pour into you. 4) Be obedient, especially when we do not understand. 5) Forgive so that your heart is free. Keep your flames high, and most importantly, do not let them go out. Find the firewood that gives you the fuel to keep going.

To Infinity and Beyond

"There are many virtuous and capable women in the world, but you surpass them all!" (Proverbs 31:29)

Who decides how far we will go in this life? Who defines us but God? Will we settle on this journey, or will we surpass (outshine, outdo, go beyond)? A woman's character is virtuous (showing high moral standards, good, respectable, godly, honest, right-minded). These are what we should aim for in the presence of God, but, yes, our flesh always trips us up. The peace we seek will help build in this type of character. God is good, and our way of living, or treating others will reflect that goodness. It is a daily battle, but we win if we are in His presence before we start each day. Also, He is particularly good at reminding us of our wrongs at the moment to save us from further damage. Be the best YOU; ask God to help you in areas you know need help. Is it selfishness, sternness, lack of compassion, or humility that pushes away the very ones He sent to help us? Be careful. With Him, there are no limits to what we can be.

December 2

Open

"Look! I stand at the door and knock. If you hear my voice and open the door, I will come in, and we will share a meal together as friends. (Revelation 3:20)

What does it take to open the door of your heart to Jesus? Some may not open their hearts because opening means messiness and brokenness will have to be dealt with and may not be ready. Some may be ashamed of past mistakes. Some may think, "Why does He want me to open? I have nothing to offer Him." Everyone has their reasons to withhold their whole hearts from Jesus. But the enemy loves it, as he knows your hand is on the knob of the door, but he keeps reminding us of the very thing that is keeping us from opening. Here it goes: open the door to your heart. He knocks because Jesus is a true gentleman and will never be forced on us to do something. We may get a little push toward His will when we resist, but that is all good. To hear Him, we need to seek Him so much that His voice is familiar. Do not allow noises to block His voice. His knock is stronger. What a true friend He is that He even knocks on our door. It is an honor to be on the receiving end, as He feels we are worth the time.

He Patiently Waited

And remember, our Lord's patience gives people time to be saved. This is what our beloved brother Paul also wrote to you with the wisdom God gave him—speaking of these things in all of his letters. Some of his comments are hard to understand, and those who are ignorant and unstable have twisted his letters to mean something quite different, just as they do with other parts of Scripture. And this will result in their destruction. (2 Peter 3:15-16)

If I tell you that it did not tug my heart as I wrote this, I would be lying. Hearts are changing, different perspectives are shared, and new identities will continue to mold. Struggles may be an inconvenience for some, but they also save some people from further self-destruction. As you continue seeking God on this journey, it will be difficult to change, but you have adjusted and will continue to adapt to all these changes. As you read, God gives us time to be saved. Amen to those who found themselves. Amen to those who made it right with others. Amen to those who now understand their identity. Amen to those who will not give the enemy another opportunity to steal their joy because they now know they have authority over him in the name of Jesus. "Thank You, Jesus, for the opportunity you gave so that the lost could find You again or finally meet you for the first time. Amen."

Never Deny Who You Are

This is a trustworthy saying: If we die with him, we will also live with him. If we endure hardship, we will reign with him. If we deny him, he will deny us. If we are unfaithful, he remains faithful, for he cannot deny who He is. (2 Timothy 2:11-13)

Sometimes to fit in, we deny our faith, but Jesus never rejected us. Perhaps as a human, He wanted to be accepted, but acceptance and others' approval cannot cause us to deny the call. Jesus had to be who He was and do what He did for hope to come. As we read in this verse, we cannot deny who He is. We live when we restrict ourselves. He is faithful even when we are not, and He will help us rise with Him in our hardships. Decide: Who are you? What do you want to accomplish in these times? Why do you tolerate what you know is not right just to be accepted by others? I pray God releases you from that position right now. Show your identity as a follower of Jesus. It is not always easy, but here is a daily reminder: "What Did Jesus Do?" It is pretty simple; whatever He does not do, we should not either. There are no excuses. Even if it is of our flesh, we deny our image in Christ. If we believe His Kingdom is not ours, maybe that is the problem.

Extending Faith

I cling to you; your strong right hand holds me securely. (Psalm 63:8)

When we extend our hands to God, we believe in all that He is and the power He alone sends down for our prayer requests. To raise your hand, you must trust and have faith; it will cause us to stretch, reach out, and endure the pain as we keep giving it to God. Cling (hold on tightly or grip) to Him. As He rescues you from your brokenness, hardships, confusion, and doubt, grip as tightly as you can. It is in the extending that answers the prayer. The verse also says that His strong right hand holds us securely. He reaches down to show He hears, knows, understands, and He will not let go. They extended their hands with faith and saw the results. Moses departed the Red Sea, and the woman who bled and merely touched Jesus was changed forever. Both had faith that change would happen, and He answered.

In Disbelief

But you do not believe me because you are not my sheep. My sheep listen to my voice; I know them, and they follow me. (John 10:26-27)

Disbelief means the inability or refusal to accept that something is true or real. We knew of Him, but we did not know Him. We did not understand what forgiveness was about until we learned that it only happens if we sincerely repent and unconditionally love. It did not sound natural, especially if we do not have people in our lives who forgive or love us like that. We now know it is accurate, and He offers more than anyone can. We know Him because we seek and hear Him. I pray for the ones in disbelief that God provides blinders (focuses on what we can see and also what we can listen to) so that they only see or hear Him. There is no direction or hope if we cannot hear or see Him working in unexplainable moments that prove His truth and promises. We believe that He leads; we follow. He speaks; we listen. He knows us as we know Him.

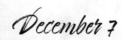

December 7

Drifting Is Not an Option

But you must continue to believe this truth and stand firmly in it. Don't drift away from the assurance you received when you heard the Good News. The Good News has been preached all over the world, and I, Paul, have been appointed as God's servant to proclaim it. (Colossians 1:23)

Sometimes our flesh stumbles. We want what we want, and we make the mistake of going ahead of God. Drifting away will happen unless you have a plan within you that alerts your mind and heart to stop and think about your next step. When we got saved, Jesus gave us comfort, love, and hope we never felt before. It was powerful, different, and we realized we only had to come as we are. We received His assurance (word of honor, promise, guarantee, vow, oath, or commitment); these are the right words. Why drift away or give it up? What God gives to us as a vow, He does not take back. Why is it hard to commit to Him like that? All He wants for us is to be happy, love each other, and help others seeking but need a little direction. Are you willing? Make a promise to follow Him, and a vow never to let anyone take His place, a commitment to study, serve, and share who He is.

Praise Him Wherever You Are

Now I say to you that you are Peter (which means 'rock'), and upon this rock I will build my church, and all the powers of hell will not conquer it. (Matthew 16:18)

I know some people feel like they need to be inside a building to praise God or feel connected to Him. Now, this is true: it is powerful to be physically present in an environment with other believers, but what God has shown us is that we can praise and pursue Him wherever we are. I pray that you have a changed mindset to increase your faith and decrease any doubts about who He is. As you read in verse, Jesus says to Peter He will build His church, and any power of hell will not conquer (overcome or take control of) it. So not even the enemy's tactics can stop us from seeking Him, praising Him, staying connected with our church family, or sharing His word with others who seek. People need and are seeking Jesus. Maybe they are resistant and need to encounter Jesus outside of a church building to help them see that they matter to Jesus too, and it is never too late.

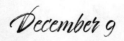

Worn Out Soul

"You're going to wear yourself out—and the people, too. This job is too heavy a burden for you to handle all by yourself. (Exodus 18:18)

God chose Moses to lead His people. If you read in Exodus, there were many times that the Israelites complained about something. Complaining is okay, but after a while, it became a burden too heavy for Moses to carry, as he was the person who heard these complaints and had direct conversations with God about them. It became a burden because it was constant. People came to him to solve issues, and he was the middleman, so he knew how God would react to any complaint. It puts a person in constant problem-solving mode, trying to fix every issue while leading alone. Leaders get worn out, it is true, but God sends who is needed to relieve them a little so that they can focus on specific assignments He gives. It does not mean they slack off. It means others will take over in certain areas or seasons as long as they have the same honorable faith and actions that focus on the truth of God. They will be just as responsible as the leader has to be. But we need to depend on people to walk this journey with us and help us carry the load.

December 10

It is About Them

I cry out to God Most High, to God who will fulfill his purpose for me. (Psalm 57:2)

We always ask God what our purpose is. But when He does reveal it, we tend to step back instead of forward and stay stagnant. Until we step forward, the ones who God has specifically chosen to come our way may be waiting on finding Him. God will always send someone else who has a willing heart to help those seeking, if not us. We wonder why our family or friends did not listen to us when we shared about Jesus and found Him when someone we knew shared a word. There can be many reasons for that, but God chooses who will be the one to help on their path, be that listening ear, be present with them, and the most beautiful part, be a witness of seeing them grow in Christ. But we will feel their pain. What you love will be a part of your purpose. There will be a cost, but you will know how to handle it, as it is unique to you. I pray that you step forward and ask God to send His people and that you are willing.

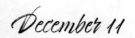

December 11

A Valued Friendship

Such wicked people are detestable to the LORD, but he offers his friendship to the godly. (Proverbs 3:32)

Friendship is so important. God offers that to us, so please take it and do not let it go. It is the primary relationship of encouragement, unconditional love, listening, and acceptance of our flaws (that He will help us work on or get rid of), but most importantly, presence. In a friendship, it is comforting to know that on our worst days, someone will take the time to listen, to be there, to share, to encourage, and to stand in the gap with strength when we are too weak to handle the hardships of life alone. God is what helps build strong friendships, as He is the central strand that keeps them together. He orchestrates who will be on our journey with us, whether in a season or forever. It is not easy, as we learn all the messy parts about each other, but we decide if those friendships are worth our hearts and time. Value them as your friendship with God, and He will bless them. May He bless all your friendships.

December 12

Exact Piece of the Puzzle

The Father and I are one." (John 10:30)

Visualize two pieces of a puzzle: one is named "unique to me," and the other is called "Holy Spirit." The one that is mine will be able to connect to other pieces of the puzzle, and the other will only connect with one piece. Once we join these two pieces, they become one piece. Jesus and God are one, and we are one with the Holy Spirit. Please understand this: we all hold a part of the puzzle with God, but that piece only connects to us personally, as we are all unique. The problem is that our selection can connect to other parts as well, but the Holy Spirit's piece only relates to us individually. Maybe we created other outlets to link to or allow others to connect because we seek this validation that only God can provide. There is a reason for that. We cannot forget that we need Him, and He is the only piece required to function in this world. To help us find life details to connect to that show us we are loved, focused, and united, God sent the Holy Spirit. Most of all, it shows us that we are never alone. Be connected today with the Holy Spirit, and your puzzle of life will make sense to you, and you will be complete.

This is Reality

The greater my wisdom, the greater my grief. To increase knowledge only increases sorrow. (Ecclesiastes 1:18)

As we seek Jesus, what is inside our hearts and minds will unravel our emotions, our curiosity, and we will get overwhelmed with joy because we will find our true selves. We see this new thing inside of us that comes alive. Why did it take so long to get to that place? How did we miss it before? Was God speaking, and we were just too busy listening to others who did not have what our souls seek? King Solomon asked God questions regarding life, and as he sought answers, he found that life is not easy. Those who try to keep Jesus out will struggle even more. Keep in mind that as we seek and find truth in Jesus, we will find our behaviors, thinking, sorrows, and, yes, selfish ways will cause us to feel bad because some of it did disrespect Jesus. But it is better to get it out now and change our ways, as He knows and is waiting for us to leave our past behind and walk into a new God-driven future. We know life struggles will still be there, but so will He.

Kept in a Bottle

You keep track of all my sorrows. You have collected all my tears in your bottle. You have recorded each one in your book. (Psalm 56:8)

God collects, keeps track, and records in His book our tears. Do we believe that? Yes, our tears are what we give to Him in prayer when the words do not come out; the tears tell the story—the story of sadness, of relief, of losing someone important to us. Answered prayers will always lead us not to hold back tears because we know only God could have answered; it means you need God's comfort, direction, and peace. Tears are not ever wasted and always cleanse the soul, and their main job will be that God will pour into other areas that need growth. God sees our tears as we surrender ourselves. He stands with us and allows us to grieve. He holds those tears and places them back into areas of the heart so that it starts His overflow and healing. Let it flow.

Just Believe

If you openly declare that Jesus is Lord and believe in your heart that God raised him from the dead, you will be saved. For it is by believing in your heart that you are made right with God, and it is by openly declaring your faith that you are saved. (Romans 10:9-10)

Here it goes: some may think that once you accept Jesus, everything will be perfect, and there will be no more hardships, brokenness, or loss, but—I am sorry—we will have all of these still. The difference is that we will not walk alone. Then what is it all about, this Jesus? This salvation? This unconditional love and forgiveness? Who does that? Why? What is there to gain? Being right with God and being saved from a world that does not give peace is what we earn. It is simple: obey, follow, know there is a cost, and not be ashamed of who you follow. How? I hear some asking. Repent of our sins, believe in our heart that Jesus is Lord and resurrected, then salvation is ours. Believing and trusting in Him will lead us to find the peace and contentment we seek. We aim to be right with God in our hearts, thinking, and actions. If the world does not see the difference in us, why would they want to seek Jesus? Say it out loud, "I believe in you, Jesus," and you will find Him.

JESUS

During my time here, I protected them by the power of the name you gave me. I guarded them so that not one was lost, except the one headed for destruction, as the Scriptures foretold. (John 17:12)

Five letters that make up a name that has saved, healed, forgiven, drawn near to the brokenhearted, restored, given grace, walked with us, led us to the right path, and, as the verse says, guarded and protected us so that no one would be lost and miss their calling. Yes, when you hear His name, you are immediately at peace, safe, comforted, encouraged, motivated and hopeful. (J)ourney: it will be one of the best you will ever travel—with bumps, yes, but never alone. (E)ternal life: it is guaranteed if we believe in Him. (S)aving: it is what He does if you open your heart and let Him in. (U)nited: what we will be in His name as we all belong to Him. (S)afe: this is being in His presence, where we are at peace, loved, accepted, needed, and given the honor to use our unique gifts to do His work. So bring others along who need Him to witness the transformation of His name.

December 17

Glorified Completion

I brought glory to you here on earth by completing the work you gave me to do. (John 17:4)

We must stop searching, questioning, excuses, or procrastinating. We are all given work that we must complete, and we know that God always gets the glory. Others thank me for the on-time daily word that I send out (I am humbled and grateful); God receives the praise all the time. As I always say, I am just a willing vessel sharing the unconditional love that I have received. I am running to spread, share, uplift, help, guide, or whatever it is doing for you. May you have that same fire inside that does not leave you alone, that tells you to get there, pray for that person, be present to be a strong tower, or whatever He gives you to do. He gets all the glory. We must claim the authority given to us. We want to be like Jesus, but we must claim our space with confidence, knowing that we go when He sends. When He opens, we walk in. When He assigns, we complete, and He always gets the glory.

Pilgrimage of Self

Dear friends, I warn you as "temporary residents and foreigners" to keep away from worldly desires that wage war against your very souls. (1 Peter 2:11)

A pilgrimage of self is going out into the world to search for something about yourself, others, or the world, and it will require going through experiences that will further understand all I mentioned. Transformation always occurs when we go out and seek what only God can reveal when we open our hearts or minds. You will have beautiful encounters. God orchestrates those moments that will be priceless and those that will be hard. Why God? For what purpose? Why the sadness? How can it be that He overflows us? We are to go out and share His hope; that is our purpose in this world. Will you jump in or sit on the sidelines? We are "temporary residents" here; our journey started when He sent us down from heaven; this is the in-between time. We need to make a difference, not waste time. Go, show who Jesus is, love, and find yourself until we get home.

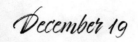

Honorable Father

Then you will again see the difference between the righteous and the wicked, between those who serve God and those who do not." (Malachi 3:18)

God says that anyone who honors Him and fears Him are His unique treasures. We are His people, but are we all in even when counting the cost? This world makes things look better than God. If others do not see the difference between believers and nonbelievers, we do not represent Jesus well in this world-this is a big problem. If not, then who are we honoring? Our ways should mirror God's ways. Did we reach out to those who needed to hear of a Savior that would change their lives? Did we change our ways rather than just going along with the world? It may be fun, but it offers no eternity in heaven. Did we encourage others that they matter even with their flaws? Did we show grace to others when they disappointed us or did we shut them down? Did we release that deep ache in our hearts that is taking away our peace? Did we let no one in because that is what we do, or did we give it to Jesus and trust Him? As He says, "let it go; it is okay now."

December 20

I Will Wait

I am counting on the LORD; yes, I am counting on him. I have put my hope in his word. (Psalm 130:5)

When we put our hope in Jesus, waiting is not a problem. By now, we know when we did not wait based on how things turned out for us. It takes a load off our back. It is saying to Jesus, "My flesh wants it now, but I know You have better things or people for me." When you have total reliance on Him, why stress? Why pressure ourselves? When we do not wait, we fall into things that fail us. Then we must start over again, and time is lost. So, what do I mean? Wait for Jesus in whatever area that you have been waiting. Pray to Him and lean into Him more. Read the Word, go to church, attend Bible study. We cannot isolate ourselves all the time. Get that spiritual food in your heart, mind, and soul. In that season, trust, hope, and try your best not to stress so that He can bless you. The cross is a reminder to trust in God's faithfulness and love.

December 21

God Shows Up

God gave these four young men an unusual aptitude for understanding every aspect of literature and wisdom. And God gave Daniel the special ability to interpret the meanings of visions and dreams. (Daniel 1:17)

There is so much in this good verse; please read all of it. Remember, we can learn anything God puts before us because He gives us the ability to master it. It will require time, thinking, resting, and pondering which way to go, but He directs by giving us peace as we step forward. Yes, we must apply ourselves to it. Daniel and three other men, who were faithful and obedient, were tested, and they passed. Are we surprised? God is for the ones who love Him. But what we need is to have confidence in knowing that He is for us in any situation—yeah, even those challenging and testing moments. God gave them an unusual aptitude (a natural ability to do something) to succeed. The Holy Spirit in us helps us comprehend things we thought we could not. We have what it takes to master anything, especially the outcome of this journey, but we must apply, trust, and go for it.

December 22

Making Effort

The more you grow like this, the more productive and useful you will be in your knowledge of our Lord Jesus Christ. (2 Peter 1:8)

Seek, and you will find. Seek knowledge by reading the Bible and listening to church leaders, believers, Bible studies, or worship music. There are so many ways that God has given us to find out about Him. Everything comes from the Bible. Please understand that in whatever way you need to connect to God, do it. The question is: What type of Christian do you want to be? The one who waits for instructions or the one who is already moving? We all have our gifts, and there is plenty to do in His Kingdom. The enemy does an excellent job of discouraging and depositing doubt in the mind that makes us feel unworthy or has us compare ourselves to others. Our minds get consumed so much that some get intimidated and step back. Jesus died for all of us to all be free from the bondage of our sins. This way, we can be helpful and productive—not only in the Word knowledge but also in our physical work and walk with Him. We need to move to reach others who do not know Him or His promises.

December 23

Entrusted More Raises the Cost

But someone who does not know, and then does something wrong, will be punished only lightly. When someone has been given much, much will be required in return; and when someone has been entrusted with much, even more will be required. (Luke 12:48)

Only God knows our breaking point. As we jump over each obstacle that comes our way, we say, "I know that He has a plan for me; I know those doors opening are the ones I need to go through; I know I have to let go of some things along the way, but I also know that You know me, Jesus." When we are tired, we do not give up. Instead, we pray for rejuvenation in the moments we are exhausted. Overthinking can be discouraging, so step into His presence so that He can take over your thoughts. Just wrestling with the cost of following Jesus can put us into a state of overthinking. But He can slow us down and bring peace. Getting closer to Him will require more of us. The cost will involve everyone we love. Some will accept it, and some will not understand the sacrifice we make due to that fire inside us, that feeling of being loved, or that secured identity that Jesus chooses us to be no matter what we lose. Others will find their way because of our obedience.

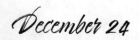

December 24

Arms Wide Open

But regarding Israel, God said, "All day long I opened my arms to them, but they were disobedient and rebellious." (Romans 10:21)

Remember this: Jesus is always waiting for us to run to Him for help, comfort, direction, or answers. What do we get out of disobedience? Rebellion? Disrespect? These are examples of what the world gives us to cling to us if the armor does not cover. When we experience the troubles of the world, is our first instinct to run to Him? He is the One we should go to for all our situations. He does not have to prove Himself; He is in control of all, especially of us. Some of us need inconvenient problems to remind us that our behaviors do not match what we say we believe; this cannot happen, as this brings confusion to others who want to believe. Run to Jesus, read about Him, learn His ways, spread who He is, and be okay in being disciplined by Him. Most likely, He is saving you from further damage.

Jesus Within

"His purpose was for the nations to seek after God and perhaps feel their way toward him and find him—though he is not far from any one of us. (Acts 17:27)

We live, move, and exist to find Him. So, what can hold us back? We have who we need that gives us strength, love, and guidance. So, start living by pouring His words into your soul for direction for your next steps. I pray that your perspective has changed to see that He can stop anything or anybody—just like that, that not even the world can stop Him. Not a negative; see it as Him helping us get back on the right track because the world's thinking always stresses our minds, as it is still running at a fast pace. Move into new mindsets, letting go of old ones that were not taking you anywhere but were overwhelming you with burdens that you do not have to carry alone. We are to exist for Him. Start doing what He expects you to do without excuses. Nothing should be blocking you from serving Him, so honestly, do what pleases Him and take care of the ones He places in your heart.

December 26

Empathetic Heart

Be happy with those who are happy, and weep with those who weep. (Romans 12:15)

Empathy means the ability to understand and share the feelings of another. Hmm, didn't Jesus do this? What would we do if He did not understand? Knowing this helps us keep going. So, when you cry, picture Him crying with you. When He blesses you with those answered prayers that only He knew, imagine Him with tears of happiness and a big smile because He knows how much it meant to you. Keep moving and aligning with His will. Here it goes: we must be like that, too. When someone weeps, our spirit should feel it and understand. Just be there without words; we do not always have to speak, but our presence speaks volumes and decreases anxieties or fears for others. Are you doing that? And when someone has joyful moments, do you join those moments with them? That is what will keep us going and is evidence of Jesus overflowing in our hearts as we extend His love to others. If someone does not share what they are going through, it is true, they will not know if we genuinely care or if we will walk with them, so I pray for God to show them it is okay to trust. God to break that spirit of discouragement that the enemy has put on others to refrain in sharing because if not, they stay trapped in their bondages.

December 27

Does it Matter to Us?

May the words of my mouth and the meditation of my heart be pleasing to you, O LORD, my rock and my redeemer. (Psalm 19:14)

Our guidance is the Holy Spirit, so what we ponder, think, do, pray, or reflect on will be filtered through Him first. If it is not good, then you will feel the difference. Is that bad? No, if we do not listen, we get ourselves in situations we have no business getting into, bringing us other issues. An example is our words: use them wisely. We will sometimes fail, but we should always aim at getting better, especially if we want to please God. Never let anyone cause you to stumble in that area. The verse says, "my Rock," which means that God is strong, solid, and unchanging. We inherit so let us start living like that. It also says, "my Redeemer," which means that only He can restore us to a place of peace, love, contentment, and only He can correct our identity, refresh our minds, or heal our hearts and souls. No one else can do this but Him. "God, thank You for restoring those areas we never thought could be fixed and for the love You embedded into our hearts so deeply. Amen."

Wanted Favor

For the LORD God is our sun and our shield. He gives us grace and glory. The LORD will withhold no good thing from those who do what is right. (Psalm 84:11)

In this verse, he reminded me that God's favor comes, that patience is essential, but when He sends it down—wow, that cup overflows. As we are trying our best to seek Him, acknowledge who He is (the driver of our soul), remain obedient to His ways, and partner with Him in helping others find their way, we grow to care about the things that are dear to Him, He sees the ones who are constantly asking, "What do I do now, Lord?" As the world tries to block His glory from others through their distractions or struggles. He sees, and He answers our prayers one by one. It is a blessing, a direction, and thank you for alternating your life to help someone else. He shines on us. He shields all areas and gives grace, but the best part is He does not withhold one good thing from us. He knows our true hearts, including sadness. "Thank you, Jesus, for blessings at the right moment."

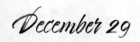

December 29

Mourn

God blesses those who mourn, for they will be comforted. (Matthew 5:4)

Mourning is a part of all our lives. We all have gone through it. It will never make sense; the only thing that does is that God walks with us each moment and keeps us standing strong while we feel like we are falling apart. God helps us through and will show up because He knows loss. Remember, Jesus was His son. He will bless and comfort—that is a promise. We will see it in time or already have. We must (M)ove forward for our loved ones, not forgetting them but honoring them by living and remembering what they poured into us. We can go to that place in our hearts and thoughts at our lowest point to help bring us up. (O)thers are sent to help us accomplish His purpose—not to replace but to hold us up in prayers. We will receive (U)nderstanding from others who know our season. (R)est in His presence is essential—to be in His hands and cry if we need to. (N)ever forget the good moments that fill our hearts and bring comfort in knowing that we were genuinely loved by those we lost.

No Talking Just Listen

My child, pay attention to what I say. Listen carefully to my words. Don't lose sight of them. Let them penetrate deep into your heart, for they bring life to those who find them, and healing to their whole body. (Proverbs 4:20-22)

God is always ahead of this world, as He knows what it will do to our thinking and our hearts. Pay attention (focus, be in tune with Him alone): many have so much to say to us but do not. The best way of handling any situation is to do what God says. Do not entertain what is not essential. He says to listen to His words and do not lose sight. Yes, it is hard for the flesh, but we want God's favor. What protects our hearts and our thinking? God's profound words, promises, and guidance are what gives us perseverance when life is not fair. God's love profoundly penetrates our hearts and minds, and nothing can damage our lives unless we lose focus. If you find contentment and God is not in the picture, how is it overflowing your cup? Hearts and thoughts not driven by God cannot bring others to Him. We have a lot of time to listen, so please hear Him.

December 31

Are We Eagerly Waiting?

And just as each person is destined to die once and after that comes judgment, so also Christ was offered once for all time as a sacrifice to take away the sins of many people. He will come again, not to deal with our sins, but to bring salvation to all who are eagerly waiting for him. (Hebrews 9:27-28)

We are eagerly waiting for Jesus. Just as we eagerly wait for a gift or a person to come, we should eagerly wait to see what God has for us. We should have this feeling daily: that eagerness to read His words or to know that what we just read ministers to our hearts—especially when we just had a conversation with God. Enthusiasm can become that drive we need to seek Him, so we do not hold back; we go for it. It is for our benefit. My sister in Christ always tells me that the more I pour into Him, the more will overflow out of me, and others will benefit by receiving the overflow. I am so grateful for her and others sharing that with me as well. Overflow is what we want, and we may or may not see that moment of how it impacts others but what we know is that God will get the glory for it, not us, as it will never be about us. This overflow fills our hearts with so much unconditional love for others that it drives us to continue to walk boldly in faith and in spreading the Good News. All He needs is a willing, unconditional love for others and an obedient heart that will go wherever He sends without questions to help the lost, hopeless, weary, discouraged, fearful, or those who have lost faith. Many people are eagerly searching in the wrong places, so Jesus has placed us in those environments so that they find hope by us sharing who He is. Let us outstretch our hands as He did for us and lead others to Him, so SALVATION happens.